The
HIDDEN PLACES
of
LANCASHIRE

*including
the Isle of Man*

*Edited by
Joanna Billing*

Published by:
Travel Publishing Ltd
7a Apollo House, Calleva Park
Aldermaston, Berks, RG7 8TN

ISBN 1-902-00715-8

© Travel Publishing Ltd 1998

First Published:	*1991*
Second Edition:	*1994*
Third Edition:	*1996*
Fourth Edition:	*1998*

Regional Titles in the Hidden Places Series:

Channel Islands	Cheshire
Cornwall	Devon
Dorset, Hants & Isle of Wight	Gloucestershire
Heart of England	Kent
Lake District & Cumbria	Lancashire
Norfolk	Northeast Yorkshire
Northumberland & Durham	Nottinghamshire
Peak District	Potteries
Somerset	South East
South Wales	Suffolk
Surrey	Sussex
Thames & Chilterns	Welsh Borders
Wiltshire	Yorkshire Dales

National Titles in the Hidden Places Series:

England	Ireland
Scotland	Wales

Printing by: Nuffield Press, Abingdon

Cartography by: Estates Publications, Tenterden, Kent

Line Drawings: Sarah Bird

Editor: Joanna Billing PPR 076794639

Cover : Clare Hackney

Born in 1961, Clare was educated at West Surrey College of Art and Design
as well as studying at Kingston University. She runs her own private water-
colour school based in Surrey and has exhibited both in the UK and ·
internationally. The cover is taken from an original water-colour of Lancaster
Castle.

Foreword

The Hidden Places series is a collection of easy to use travel guides taking you, in this instance, on a relaxed but informative tour through Lancashire and the Isle of Man. Our books contain a wealth of interesting information on the history, the countryside, the towns and villages and the more established places of interest. But they also promote the more secluded and little known visitor attractions and places to stay, eat and drink many of which are easy to miss unless you know exactly where you are going.

We include hotels, inns, restaurants, public houses, teashops, various types of accommodation, historic houses, museums, gardens, garden centres, craft centres and many other attractions throughout Lancashire and the Isle of Man. Most places have an attractive line drawing and are cross-referenced to coloured maps found at the rear of the book. We do not award merit marks or rankings but concentrate on describing the more interesting, unusual or unique features of each place with the aim of making the reader's stay in the local area an enjoyable and stimulating experience.

Whether you are visiting the area for business or pleasure or in fact are living in the county we do hope that you enjoy reading and using this book. We are always interested in what readers think of places covered (or not covered) in our guides so please do not hesitate to use the reader reaction forms provided to give us your considered comments. We also welcome any general comments which will help us improve the guides themselves. Finally if you are planning to visit any other corner of the British Isles we would like to refer you to the list of other *Hidden Places* titles to be found at the rear of the book.

Contents

CHAPTER ONE
North Lancashire and the Forest of Bowland

Clougha Pike

Chapter 1 - Area Covered

For precise location of places please refer to the colour maps found at the rear of the book.

1
North Lancashire and the Forest of Bowland

Introduction

The county of Lancashire is known to many people but, perhaps, more than any other area in the country it has suffered from cliched images of its landscape and people: the harsh life of the mill towns and the brashness of Blackpool. Before the reorganization of the county boundaries in 1974, this large area also included Liverpool and Manchester in the south and the Furness Peninsula to the north. Though each, with their own distinctive character, were lost, the Red Rose county, which has put many a king on the throne of England, has much more besides.

As the well-known Lancashire comedian, Les Dawson, commented in his book on the county, it is 'many things to many people' with 'vast smoky grey blocks of heavy industry' but also a countryside of 'lakes and woods and rolling hills'. It is also a place of great history: the Wars of the Roses; the old Catholic families and their support of Charles I during the Civil War; the trials of the Pendle Witches; and the innovators that started the Industrial Revolution in the textile industry.

The ancient county town of Lancaster, in the north, is an excellent place to start any journey of discovery. With a variety of museums and a wealth of interesting buildings, the life of Lancastrians through the ages is mapped out for any visitor to explore. Small and compact, it has the added advantage of having been off the general tourist routes which has made its larger, White Rose equivalent, somewhat hard going in the height of the season.

To the northeast lies Leck Fell, just south of Kirkby Lonsdale and Cumbria. It is easy for the visitor to mistake this for the Yorkshire Dales as there is a typical craggy limestone gorge along the little valley of Leck Beck, as well as one of the most extensive cave systems in the British Isles for the experienced potholer to explore. A natural route from Kirkby Lonsdale back to the county town is marked by the River Lune. For those who enjoy walking, the best way to enjoy this wonderful green and hilly area of Lancashire is to follow the **Lune Valley Ramble** which travels the valley's intimate pastoral setting, through woodland, meadows, and along the riverside itself.

To the west of Lancashire lies Morecambe Bay, a treacherous place, where over the centuries, many walkers have lost their lives in an attempt to make the journey to the Furness Peninsula considerably shorter. Walks across the sands, at low tide, should only be undertaken with the aid of one of the highly knowledgeable and experienced guides. However, despite it grim history, the bay offers superb views, including glorious sunsets, as well as being an important habitat for a wide variety of birds.

Extending across much of the north of the county is the Forest of Bowland, an ancient royal hunting ground that is dotted with small, isolated villages. With no major roads passing through the area, it has remained little changed and, with so many splendid walks and fine countryside, it is also relatively quiet even during the busiest summer weeks.

Lancaster

The capital of this beautiful county, Lancaster proudly boasts of its legacy, which extends back many centuries. Unlike York its White Rose cousin, which has long been internationally known as a tourist attraction, this Red Rose city has taken longer to be discovered. In fact, Lancaster has an equally important place in English history and it has retained close links with the monarchy. As early as the 10th century, Athelstan, the grandson of Alfred the Great, had lands in the area and it was during the reign of William the Conqueror that large areas of what is now Lancashire were given, by the grateful king, to his cousin Roger of Pitou, who made his base at Lancaster. The first Earl of Lancaster was Edmund, the youngest son of Henry III and, in time, the title passed to John of Gaunt who persuaded

Richard II to give him the right to pass the title on to his highest male descendent. Now a dukedom, to this day the present Queen still retains the title of Duke of Lancaster.

There is much in this historic place for the serious visitor to explore and, as it is also a surprisingly compact city, easily reached by either road, just off the M6, or by rail, it is also a pleasure.

Within yards of the railway station lies **Lancaster Castle**, a great medieval fortress, founded by the Normans to keep out Scottish invaders, and strengthened by John of Gaunt, Duke of Lancaster, in the 15th century. Standing proudly on its hilltop position, this great castle has an imposing presence and dominates the skyline over Lancaster. Its huge square keep dates back to 1200 and was raised in height and impregnability at the time of the Armada. Astonishingly perhaps, most of the building still functions as a prison, but certain sections are open to the public, including the 18th century **Shire Hall**, the cells where the witches of Pendle were

Lancaster Castle

5

imprisoned, and the **Crown Court**. The Crown Court not only saw the trials of the Pendle witches but also those of John Paslew (last abbot of Whalley) in 1536, numerous Catholic priests during the 16th and early 17th centuries, and, more recently, the Birmingham pub bombers in 1975. Hadrian's Tower and - a touch of the macabre - the Drop Room where prisoners were prepared for the gallows can also be viewed by the public.

Close by, sharing the hill with the castle, is a building with less grim associations - the lovely **Priory Church of St Mary**; which once served a Benedictine Priory established here in 1094. Most of the present church dates from the 14th and 15th centuries and of particular interest here are the fragments of Anglo-Saxon crosses, the magnificent medieval choir stalls, and some very fine needle-work. The **Priory Tower**, also on the hilltop, was rebuilt in 1759 as a landmark for ships navigating their way into the River Lune. Nearby is one of Lancaster's links with its Roman past - the re-mains of a bath house which also served soldiers as an inn.

A short walk from the castle leads into the largely pedestrian-ised city centre, full of shops, the market, and much besides. The **City Museum** in the Market Place occupies the Old Town Hall, built between 1781-3 by Major Jarrett and Thomas Harrison. As well as the city's art collection and an area of changing exhibitions, there are displays and collections of material illustrating aspects of the city's industrial and social history. Also here is the **Museum of the King's Own Royal Regiment**, a regiment which was based in Lan-caster from 1880 onwards.

In Church Street is the **Judge's Lodging**, a beautifully propor-tioned building dating from the 1620s when it was originally built as a private house for Thomas Covell then, later, used by judges during the Lancaster Assizes. It now houses two separate muse-ums: the **Museum of Childhood** containing the Barry Elder doll collection; and the **Gillow and Town House Museum** containing many examples of the fine workmanship of Gillows, the famous Lancaster cabinet-makers. In fact, it was Richard Gillow who de-signed the city's Maritime Museum. Close by is the **Cottage Museum** in a house, built in 1739, that was divided into two dwell-ings in the 19th century. Furnished in the style of an artisan's house of the early to mid-19th century, the museum is open from Easter to the end of September. Just around a corner or two, in Sun Street, is the **Music Room**, an exquisite early Georgian building originally designed as a pavilion in the long vanished garden of Oliver Marton. It is notable for some superb decorative plasterwork.

Lancaster grew up along the banks of the River Lune, which is navigable as far as Skerton Bridge, so there has always been a strong association between the town and its watery highway. Documents from 1297 make reference to the town's small-scale maritime trade, but it was not until the late 17th and early 18th centuries that Lancaster's character as a port fully emerged. The splendid buildings of the 18th century Golden Age were born out of the port wealth, and the layout and appearance of the town was much altered by this building bonanza. Lancaster as a port gradually declined throughout the 19th century so that many buildings put up for specific maritime purposes were taken over for other uses. Naturally, the city has been affected by the arrival of the Lancaster Canal, the railways, and 19th century industry; yet the hallmark of Lancaster, its Georgian centre, remains as the product of this maritime prosperity.

Lancaster's rich maritime history is celebrated at *St George's Quay* which, with its great stone warehouses and superb *Custom House*, is now an award-winning *Maritime Museum*. In Georgian times this was a thriving port with the warehouses receiving ship loads of mahogany, tobacco, rum, and sugar from the West Indies. Visitors today are given a vivid insight into the life of the mariners and quayside workers, with opportunities for knot-tying and the practising of other maritime skills. Every year, over the four days of the Easter weekend, St George's Quay is home to the Lancaster Maritime Festival with smugglers, sea songs, and shanties.

Built between 1797 and 1819, the *Lancaster Canal* stretches 57 miles from Preston through the centre of Lancaster to Kendal. Today, it is navigable between Preston and Tewitfield, north of Lancaster, the longest lock-free stretch of canal in the country. The canal offers a diversity of scenery and wildlife with opportunities for long-distance trips and short, circular walks with fine views through peaceful countryside. With 41 lock-free miles it offers relaxed boating with canalside pubs, restaurants, and boat-hire facilities. It provides a good touring route for canoeists and is excellent for coarse fishing.

One of the first sights visitors see of the city is the great green copper dome of the impressive *Ashton Memorial*, a landmark for miles around. A kind of miniature St Paul's - standing on a hilltop in the centre of the wonderful Edwardian *Williamson Park* - this is a magnificent viewpoint from which Morecambe Bay, the Lakeland Hills, and the Forest of Bowland are all visible. The building now houses exhibitions and multi-screen presentations about the life and

Ashton Memorial

times of Lancaster's Lord Ashton and the Edwardians. The park and the memorial all commemorate the life and works of Lancaster's most famous son, James Williamson. He was born in the town in 1842 and took over the running of the family business, linoleum and textile manufacture, which went on to become Lancaster's largest employer. Williamson was the Liberal MP for the town for many years and, in 1895, he became Lord Ashton.

Williamson Park was Lord Ashton's own personal idea as a means of providing work for local people during the cotton famine crisis in the textile industry during the American Civil War in the 1860s. Constructed on the site of old quarries, which gives the park its undulating contours, the park was opened in 1896. As well as the magnificent Ashton Memorial there is also a delightful **Butterfly House** in the now restored Edwardian Palm House and the Conservation Garden and Wildlife Pool, which opened in 1991.

Another place the whole family can enjoy is **Lancaster Leisure Park** on Wyresdale Road. Set in 42 acres of landscaped parkland, the site includes a mini-marina, a Wild West adventure playground, a miniature railway, a rare breeds unit, a children's farmyard, pony rides, a gift shop, a tea garden, and a pottery shop.

Situated in the heart of Lancaster and housed in a building which dates back to 1797, *Joseph's Restaurant* is an excellent place that is well worth finding. Since owners, Elizabeth and José Granados, opened the restaurant in 1990, they have gained an enviable reputation for the high quality of their delicious home-cooked cuisine

Joseph's Restaurant

and also for an ambience that is uniquely theirs. Though the premises are small and cosy, the restaurant is big on atmosphere and the very Continental decor, including the tiled floor and soft lighting, gives it a superb feel that complements the cuisine as well as making the whole dining experience here enjoyable.

Open every day except Sundays, Joseph's Restaurant has a range of menus that cater to the needs of its customers from first thing in the morning to well into the evening. As well as serving morning coffee and afternoon tea, there is a light lunch menu and, for the evening, a table d'hôte and an à la carte menu. All these are supplemented by an ever-changing list of daily specials that make full use of the freshest ingredients available at the local market. José is the chef of the partnership and the delicious dishes he creates reflect the cosmopolitan atmosphere of the restaurant. All beautifully prepared and presented, any meal here is sure to be a delightful dining experience. Not surprisingly, Joseph's Restaurant is popular with both locals and visitors alike and, particularly in the evening, it is necessary to book to avoid disappointment. Customers should also remember that the restaurant has a no smoking policy. *Joseph's Restaurant, 10 Gage Street, Lancaster, Lancashire LA1 1UH Tel: 01524 844707*

Right in the heart of the town and adjacent to the indoor shopping centre, *Ruxton's* is the ideal place to stop for a drink and a bit to eat whilst out in Lancaster. The pub has been managed since 1995 by Maria Livesey and she and her staff ensure that anyone dropping in can be sure of some excellent refreshment as well as a warm welcome and a relaxing time. There are the usual ales and

Ruxton's

beers served at the bar and anything from a tasty sandwich to a juicy steak is on the all-day menu. Up until the 1960s, this lively town centre pub was known as The Boar's Head but it changed its name to Ruxton's, in memory of one of Lancaster's more infamous citizens. A well-liked local general practitioner, Ruxton was found guilty of murdering his wife and her maid and was hanged in Strangeways prison in 1936. A corner of the pub is dedicated to this gentleman and photographs and other memorabilia tell this grisly tale. *Ruxton's, 20-22 Great John Street, Lancaster, Lancashire LA1 1NG Tel: 01524 34620*

Found tucked away in Music Room Square is the delightful **Sunbury Coffee House**, which has been owned and personally run by Gill and John Constable since 1992. Housed in a listed building that dates from 1798, the Georgian theme extends from the attractive stone façade to the elegant interior with its marble table tops and this provides the perfect setting in which to enjoy the fine selection of teas and coffees accompanied by the delicious freshly prepared snacks. A diverse range of coffees are always available, including Colombian, Kenyan Blue Mountain, Costa Rica, New Guinea, Old Government Java, and decaffeinated, and there is an equally fine range of teas. The food too is excellent and ranges from open sandwiches and savoury filled croissants to filled jacket pota-

Sunbury Coffee House

toes, not to mention the mouth-watering display of home-made cakes and pastries. All in all, Sunbury Coffee House is a very tempting stopping off point for those discovering the delights of this historic town. *Sunbury Coffee House, Music Room Square, 28 Sun Street, Lancaster, Lancashire LA1 1EW Tel: 01524 843312*

Situated along the banks of the Lancaster Canal, **The Navigation** wine bar and bistro is a superb establishment owned and run by Clive Bennison. When he first bought the premises, it was little more than a white-washed workshop and storeroom at the place where water was extracted from the canal and used to generate electrical power for Lancaster. Today, the scene could not be more different. The wine bar offers customers a true flavour of the Continent. Its delicious menu, created by Greg the chef, is continental but the setting can only be described as tropical. The atmospheric bar leads into a large room, the main dining area, which is not only home to several trees and shrubs but also Oscar, a blue and gold South American Macaw who is always happy to exchange banter with customers. The wine bar and bistro is open all day during the summer and during the evening in winter.

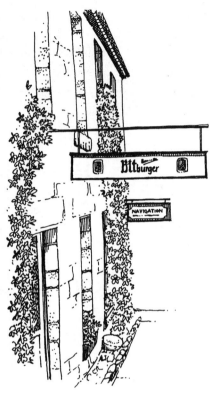

The Navigation

Not only is The Navigation famous for its fine food, wine, and beer, as well as its unique atmosphere, but Clive also offers canal cruises on his narrowboat. During the season, the boat travels along a 4-mile stretch of the Lancaster Canal which includes the impressive Lune Aqueduct that was built in 1797 by John Rennie. All in all, The Navigation is certainly one of the places of interest in Lancaster that is not to be missed. *The Navigation, Penny Street Bridge Wharf, Lancaster, Lancashire LA1 1XN Tel: 01524 849484*

Just over a mile south from the centre of Lancaster, in **Bowerham**, is the **Fox and Goose** pub that is ably managed by Jackie and Tim. Open seven days a week and all day on Fridays, Saturdays, and Sundays, this pleasant establishment serves a range of ales, beers, lagers, and ciders as well as tasty bar snacks and meals all in a quiet and relaxing setting. Though the building is relatively new, it was built in the 1950s, the Fox and Goose is full of atmosphere with live music on Wednesday evenings, quizzes on

Fox and Goose

Tuesday nights, and all the usual pub games are enthusiastically played. Popular with locals, the peaceful setting and warm welcome offered to children, make this a great place for those to visit whilst touring north Lancashire. *Fox and Goose, Newlands Road, Bowerham, Lancaster, Lancashire LA1 4JF Tel: 01524 66899*

North of Lancaster

Halton   *Map 4 ref D4*
2 miles N of Lancaster off A683

The high mound, **Castle Hill**, which rises above this ancient village, was, firstly, the site of a Roman camp, and later a Saxon castle. The village's parish **Church of St Wilfrid** was founded in the 7th century and, although nothing can be seen from that time, there are some stone crosses, both inside the building and out, that date from the 9th century. One in particular bears both pagan and Christian symbols and it is the only known cross to do so. Roman remains, in the form of a votive altar (where offerings were made before a military operation began), were found on the site in the late 18th century.

Dating back to the late 18th century, **The Greyhound** is an old coaching inn on the main road through this quiet village. Though these extensive premises have been modernised over the years to give customers the most up-to-date facilities, the refurbishments have been sympathetic and in keeping with the age and character of the inn. The wood panelled walls, tiled floors, and leaded windows remain and there is plenty of comfortable seating for everyone.

The Greyhound

The pub has been managed since 1997 by Cheryl and Bob Sutton, experienced licensees with over 25 years in the trade, and it is due to them and their chef, Mike Rawes, that The Greyhound established itself as a superb place for good food and drink in pleasant, friendly surroundings. Open all day, every day, as well as the well-stocked bar, a tasty menu of home-cooked dishes is offered to customers, supplemented by the daily specials board, that is sure to tempt everyone. During the summer, visitors can also make use of the excellent beer garden and children are welcome at all times. Due to its popularity, it is advisable to book a table at the weekends. *The Greyhound, 10 Low Road, Halton, near Lancashire LA2 6LZ Tel: 01524 811356*

Nether Kellet   *Map 4 ref D3*
4 miles N of Lancaster off B6254

This farming village has a traditional village green which, as well as being the central focus of the community, also features several old wells and pumps. Quarrying too has taken place here for many centuries and lime burning has been an important local industry. Its remains, in the form of lime kilns, can still be seen around the village.

Carnforth   *Map 4 ref D3*
5 miles N of Lancaster on A6

The town lies around what was once a major crossroads on the A6 but it is, perhaps, its fame as a busy railway junction town - whose station was used as the setting for the 1940s film classic *Brief Encounter* - by which most people known Carnforth. Though the station has declined in importance, now an unstaffed halt, the old engine sheds and sidings are occupied by **Steamtown**, one of the largest steam railway centres in the north of England. Visitors are likely to see such giants of the Age of Steam as the Flying Scotsman or an A4 Pacific being stabled here, together with a permanent collection of over 30 British and Continental steam locomotives. There are steam rides in the summer months on both standard gauge and miniature lines.

Yealand
Map 4 ref D2

8 miles N of Lancaster off A6

To the south of the village lies **Leighton Hall** - a fine early 19th-century house which is open to the public. In the Middle Ages, this land, and much of the surrounding area, was owned by the d'Avranches family. Over the centuries, the house and the land passed through many hands before becoming the property of the Gillows family of Lancaster. Now in the hands of the Reynolds family, a branch of the Gillows, the fine furniture seen in the hall reflects the trade that made the family fortune.

As with many estates in Lancashire, Leighton Hall was a Catholic house and, one owner, Sir George Middleton, was fined heavily by Cromwell after the Civil War for his loyalty to Charles I and to his religion. Later, another owner of the hall, Albert Hodgson, suffered for his loyalty to Catholicism and the Stuart claim on the throne of England. Taking part in the Jacobite rebellion of 1715, Hodgson was captured at Preston and the Government troops inflicted such damage on the hall that little remained of the Tudor structure.

The hall, today, dates from 1800 when it was built out of pale, local sandstone to the Gothic designs of Harrison, a Chester architect. One of the finest houses in the county, the views from the extensive grounds are magnificent and take in the nearby **Leighton Moss Bird Reserve**.

Silverdale
Map 4 ref D2

8 miles N of Lancaster off A6

The village lies at the northwesternmost corner of the county and has the Lakeland hills as a backdrop as well as superb views over Morecambe Bay. The latter half of the 19th century saw Silverdale develop as a quiet seaside resort where those so inclined could take medicinal baths of fresh sea water in one of the many small villas situated along the coast. One frequent visitor was Elizabeth Gaskell who is said to have written at least part of all her books whilst holidaying here.

However, Silverdale's history goes back well beyond the days of a genteel Victorian resort. Its name comes from a Viking family which settled here and which signifies that this was Sigward's or Soevers' valley. Fishing, naturally, was the key provider of local income, but in the 18th century, a copper smelting works was built here. All, however, that remains of the foundry is the chimney near **Jenny Brown's Point**, said to be named after an old woman who lived here in the 18th century.

Essentially, now a small residential village, Silverdale is well worth visiting for the network of footpaths from here that pass through the limestone woodlands that are such a joy for the botanist, being rich in wild flowers in spring - primroses, violets, orchids, bird's eye primroses, rockroses, and eglantines abound.

Leighton Moss near Silverdale is a nationally known RSPB bird sanctuary. The reed beds are the most important part of the reserve because they have become a northern stronghold of the rare bearded tit and are also the major British breeding centre for the bittern.

Whittington

Map 4 ref E2

12 miles NE of Lancaster on B6254

This delightful village, in the green and sheltered valley of the River Lune, is well worth a visit. It was Wordsworth, in his *Guide to the Lakes*, who recommended that Kendal be approached via the Vale of Lune and it remains a popular place today.

The Dragon's Head dates back to the days of the mailcoaches when it was built by James Burrows. On becoming a pub and hotel a short time later, the intention was to name it after the local Lord of the Manor, North, but he refused to give his permission, so the inn took its present name, as a dragon's head appears on the North coat of arms.

In keeping with the age of the premises, the interior has an olde worlde atmosphere, is pleasantly decorated, and there is a fine display of old sporting equipment. Run by Hazel and Chris Tomkins, the Dragon's Head has plenty to offer its customers. Not only is there a fine selection of real ales and wine by the glass from the bar, but a delicious menu of tasty bar snacks and meals are served at both lunchtime and in the evening.

Guests wishing to extend their stay at the Dragon's Head have a choice of two comfortable bedrooms which are let on a bed and breakfast basis and there is also a field at the rear of the hotel, that takes up to five touring caravans. Also found behind the building is an

The Dragon's Head

excellent piste where the French game, Petanque, is enthusiastically played by customers. *The Dragon's Head, Whittington, Nr
Kirkby Lonsdale, Carnforth, Lancashire LA6 2NY Tel: 01524272383*

Cowan Bridge
Map 4 ref F2

13 miles NE of Lancaster on A65

The school attended by the Brontë sisters, and immortalised in *Jane
Eyre* as Lowood, can still be seen though it is now part of a row of
terraced cottages. The school, which moved to Casterton in 1833,
was founded some 10 years earlier by Carus Wilson, the vicar of
neighbouring Tunstall. His rather plain house can still be seen here.

Leck
Map 4 ref F2

13 miles NE of Lancaster off A65

Over the A65 from Cowan Bridge lies the small village of Leck. To
the northeast of this village lies **Green Hill**, surrounded by moorland and the highest point, at 2,060 feet, in the county. At just over
three feet higher than the top of the neighbouring fell, Gragarth, it
was only a recent, more accurate survey, that distinguished Green
Hill as the higher. In the northernmost part of Lancashire, from
the summit there are superb views of both Cumbria and North Yorkshire, as well, of course, as Lancashire.

Tunstall
Map 4 ref E3

11 miles NE of Lancaster on A683

The village is famous for its **Church of St John the Baptist**, that was known to the Brontë sisters and which is referred to in *Jane Eyre* as Brocklebridge. It is easily forgotten that, though the Brontë family will, forever, be linked with Haworth, West Yorkshire, not only did the sisters know Tunstall but they also attended a school for clergymen's daughters at Cowan Bridge, just a few miles further north. However, the church has other features that are worthy of investigation. Over the church porch is a reminder of the bravery the men of the Lune Valley showed against the Scots at the Battle of Flodden in 1513.

Hornby
Map 4 ref E3

8 miles NE of Lancaster on A683

The situation of this village, by a bluff overlooking the valley of the River Lune, not only gives Hornby panoramic views of the surrounding countryside but also makes this a strategic position that has been utilised over the centuries. Just to the north of the village is the attractive stone-built **Loyn Bridge**, which takes the road over the River Lune and on to Gressington. Constructed in 1684, it replaced a ford and beside the bridge is **Castle Stede**, the best example of a Norman motte and bailey castle in Lancashire.

The romantically situated **Hornby Castle**, which can be viewed from the village, was immortalised in a painting by Turner. Although it was only built in the 19th century, the castle incorporates the ruins of an older castle and is now a grand and picturesque country house.

The Church of St Margaret of Antioch dates from around 1300 when it was built as a chapel of easy to the parish church at Melling. The octagonal tower is said to have been ordered by Sir Edward Stanley after the victory of Flodden Field in 1513.

Claughton
Map 4 ref E3

6 miles NE of Lancaster on A683

The **Old Toll House Garage**, on the road into this village (which is pronounced Clafton), is famous as a garage owner, earlier this century, painted the first white lines on the road at the nearby corner because of the many accidents that had occurred there. After much debate their value was recognised by George V and from then onwards the use of white lines became accepted as a means of road marking, eventually spreading world-wide.

Caton
Map 4 ref E4

3 miles NE of Lancaster on A683

Just to the south of the village, tucked away among the hills on the northern edges of the Forest of Bowland, is **Littledale**, one of Lancashire's more hidden gems. Chiefly wooded, a walk along Artle Beck, to Littledale Hall, many of the buildings of which were built in the mid-19th century by John Dodson, vicar of Cockerham, is well worthwhile and provides a view of Lancashire that is not normally seen.

West of Lancaster

Morecambe
Map 4 ref C4

3 miles NW of Lancaster on A589

Featuring prominently on the Lancashire coastline, Morecambe has long been one of the most successful and popular seaside resorts in the North, and it can truly be said to enjoy one of the finest views from its promenade of any resort in England - a magnificent sweep of coastline and bay, looking across to the Lakeland mountains. Like other resorts, Morecambe has changed with the times, and major new attractions include the multi-million pound Bubbles Leisure Park and Superdome, as well as a Wild West Theme Park. WOMAD, Morecambe's annual world music festival, attracts visitors from across the globe. There are also popular seafront illuminations in late summer, together with all the usual lively shops and variety of entertainment associated with a busy seaside resort.

However, Morecambe is a relatively recent town, that grew up as a direct result of the expansion of the railways to the north Lancashire coast. Originally three villages, Bare, Poulton, and Torrisholme that were quiet fishing communities, in 1848 all this changed as the railways brought visitors from the textile towns of Lancashire, and especially Yorkshire, to what was jokingly called 'Bradford-by-the-Sea'. Hotels and boarding houses were built as well as the usual seaside amenities, such as parks and promenades, and soon the villages were lost into one thriving resort.

Of the many buildings dating from Morecambe's heyday as a holiday destination, one in particular, the **Midland Hotel** stands out. Situated on the seafront, at the southern end of the promenade, the hotel, which was built in the early 1930s to designs by Oliver Hill, is concave towards the sea and convex facing inland. The elegant, sweeping balconies of the luxurious rooms remain a superb feature of the hotel and, whilst filming *Brief Encounter*, at nearby Carnforth, both Celia Johnson and Trevor Howard made their home here along with others working on the film.

The railway also turned Morecambe into a thriving port and, in the mid-19th century it was handling twice as much cargo as Glasson Dock. However, in the same way as it had outgrown its neighbour, Heysham, the docks in the town further south again took over and the port of Morecambe died as quickly as they had grown. Fortunately, though, the local delicacy, shrimps, that were so loved by the Victorians with their afternoon tea, are still available and they make a delicious savoury dish.

Morecambe Bay, a vast wide, flat tidal plain, situated between Lancashire and Cumbria is the home of many forms of marine life as well as being a very popular and important habitat for birds. The Rivers Lune, Kent, Keer, Leven, and Crayke create the gulleys, mud, and sandbanks that make this not only one of the most important ornithological sites in Europe but also a great source of mussels and shrimps. It is also a treacherous place for the unwary as, though it looks a simple walk across the bay, the sands are extremely hazardous and a crossing should not be made, in any circumstances, without the direct supervision of a sand pilot. Over the centuries, many have perished whilst attempting the crossing and, at one time, the monks of the Furness peninsula acted as guides to those wishing to make their way to Cumbria without taking the long overland route.

Heysham   Map 4 ref C4
5 miles W of Lancaster on A683

It is worth strolling along the promenade in a southerly direction as far as Heysham, Morecambe's twin, with its quaint old main street that winds down to the shore. It is also a town with considerable historic associations, because it was here in the 8th century that Christian missionaries arrived from Ireland to convert the heathen Viking settlers in the north of England. They built the chapel of St Patrick on a rock on the sea edge and it is likely that this is the county's oldest religious house. Its ruins, with coffin-shaped rocks - one of the most curious graveyards in England - can still be seen.

The little **Church of St Peter** on the headland below the chapel is equally interesting. It dates back to Saxon and Norman times, with an Anglo-Saxon cross on which the Madonna and other figures have been crudely carved by 9th century masons, and there is a rare Viking hog-back gravestone. It is one of the oldest churches in western Europe to have been in continuous use.

Alongside these antiquities is the modern port of Heysham, with regular car-ferry sailings to the Isle of Man and to Northern Ireland and, of course, the two modern nuclear power stations, Heysham A and Heysham B.

Sunderland   *Map 4 ref C5*
6 miles SW of Lancaster off A683

This is, unbelievably, an old port and seaside resort, which flourished until larger-berthed ships, silting channels, and the growth last century of rail-served Morecambe caused it to decline. A little wharf, quiet cottages, some with faded and evocative elegance, a sandy shore where sea thrift flourishes among the pebbles, are all that remains. The River Lune estuary is now a Site of Special Scientific Interest because of its wildlife value - visitors are likely to see such birds as redshank feeding on the rich food supplies of worms, shellfish, and shrimps on the saltmarshes, while a variety of wildfowl such as shelduck, wigeon, and mallard, are to be seen in autumn.

A particularly sad story acts as a reminder of Sunderland's time as a port. Sambo was a sea captain's servant at the time of the slave trade into Lancaster, who probably died of a fever in 1736 after a long and difficult voyage from the West Indies. Because he was not a baptised Christian, Sambo was not allowed to be buried in consecrated ground. In later years, his death and grave, marked by a simple cross and stone, became a potent local symbol of the anti-slavery cause.

His grave can be still seen, in a field at the west side of Sunderland Point. It can be reached by walking along The Lane from the village foreshore, past Upsteps Cottage where Sambo died, and turning left at the shore then over a stile on the left which gives access to the simple gravestone. Fresh flowers are usually to be seen here, mysteriously placed on the grave.

South of Lancaster

Glasson   *Map 4 ref D5*
4 miles SW of Lancaster on B5290

On the opposite side of the Lune estuary from Sunderland Point (and only reached by a long road journey through Lancaster) is **Glasson Dock**. The silting of the River Lune that ended Lancaster's importance as a port was the reason for the building of this dock in 1787 which held 25 sea-going ships and traded extensively in slaves, rum, tobacco, sugar, and cotton. In 1825, a branch of the

Lancaster Canal was built to provide a better link between the city and the docks, and this was, in turn, supplemented by a railway line in 1883. This railway is now the footpath and cycle-way to Lancaster's St George's Quay.

However, the village has not lost touch with boats and it is now a sailing centre, with the old canal basin a popular marina, and the old wharves and warehouses transformed into an attractive leisure area, with pubs and shops serving a different kind of sea-going clientele.

From Glasson there is a footpath along the coast to Plover Scar, where a lighthouse guards the River Lune estuary, and further along lie the ruins of **Cockersand Abbey**. The abbey was founded in 1190 by the Premonstratensian Order on the site of a hospital that had been the home of a hermit, Hugh Garth, before becoming a colony for lepers and the infirm. The Chapter House of the abbey remains as it was a burial chapel for the Daltons of Thurnham, descendants of Sir Thomas Moore.

Thurnham   Map 4 ref D4
5 miles S of Lancaster on A588
Just outside the village and down a sweeping drive lies **Thurnham Hall**, which has been built, over the years, around a 14th century pele tower. The home of the Dalton family for 400 years, they were responsible for the Elizabethan extensions and a fine Jacobean staircase. Still in private hands and not open to the public, although the hall has been divided up into flats much of its original character has been retained.

Galgate   Map 4 ref D5
4 miles S of Lancaster on A6
Situated on the banks of the River Conder, the village still contains some of its original mills, though they have now been put to other uses.

Bay Horse   Map 4 ref D5
6 miles S of Lancaster off the A6
The Fleece Inn, found on the main road through the village of Bay Horse to the south of Lancaster - just off junction 33 of the M6 for those travellers who might wish to break a journey - is an attractive late 18th century pub that has been managed by Liz and Peter from the beginning of 1998. Open seven days a week this is an inn well worth finding as not only are there a fine selection of real ales, beers, and lagers on tap but The Fleece Inn has an excellent reputation for

The Fleece Inn

the delicious meals that are served both at lunchtime and in the evening. So well known and popular is its cosy restaurant that it is now becoming increasingly necessary to book a table at the weekends. As well as the intimate dining area, meals and bar snacks are also served in the comfortable bar areas that are decorated in a style reminiscent of late Victorian parlour. With such a wonderful atmosphere, good food and ale, and a warm and friendly welcome, it is not surprising that The Fleece Inn is a popular choice with both locals and visitors alike. In addition to the facilities at the pub, there is also a caravan site, with six berths, behind the inn that is open all year round. *The Fleece Inn, Bay Horse, near Lancaster, Lancashire LA2 9AQ Tel: 01524 791233*

Cockerham   *Map 4 ref D5*
6 miles S of Lancaster on A588
Home to Cockerham Hall, a fine and rare example of a medieval timber-framed building that dates from the late 15th century, the village is also famous for its local custom of fluke fishing.

Standing in the heart of some of the best countryside Lancashire has to offer, **Moss Wood Caravan Park** has to be one of the most picturesque camping sites in the county. Founded 25 years ago, this family-run site covers some 28 acres in total of which just over half is set aside for both permanent holiday homes and touring caravans. All the touring pitches have hard standing and electricity supplies and the whole area has been landscaped to give holidaymakers privacy and seclusion. As well as the well-equipped site

Moss Wood Caravan Park

shop, modern shower and toilet block, children's play area, and recreation field, a large area of this tree-lined park has been left as
woodland through which there are a number of trails. This charming, well-maintained site has been the proud winner of the David
Bellamy Environmental Award for the past two years. Convenient
for many of the attractions of north Lancashire, as well as the National Parks of the Yorkshire Dales and the Lake District, Moss Wood
is open from April to October. *Moss Wood Caravan Park, Crimbles
Lane, Cockerham, Lancashire LA2 0ES Tel: 01524 791041 Fax:
01524 792444*

East of Lancaster

Quernmore   *Map 4 ref E4*
3 miles E of Lancaster off A683
Lying at the head of the Conder Valley, this farming village had a
pottery industry as well as slate quarrying in the 17th century. The
word 'quern' refers to a particularly ancient form of hand-mill that
was hewn from the rocks found on the nearby moorside and, indeed, corn milling continued here until World War II.

To the east of the village lies ***Clougha Pike***, itself on the western edges of the Forest of Bowland Area of Outstanding Natural
Beauty and one of the few places in the area that is accessible to
walkers. Although it is not the highest peak in the forest - it is just
over 1300 feet - the walk up Clougha Pike is very pleasant and one
which offers splendid views at the summit, not only of the Lakeland
Fells but also of Morecambe Bay and, on a clear day, Blackpool Tower.

Clougha Pike

Lee   Map 4 ref E5
7 miles SE of Lancaster off A6

To the northwest of this typical Bowland village lies the highest
summit in the forest, **Ward's Stone**. Dotted with outcrops of
gritstone boulders, the top of the fell is marked by two triangulation
pillars: one of which is just over three feet higher than the other
though, on first inspection, they look the same height. The panoramic views from this point are magnificent and, to the north and
east, the Three Peaks of Yorkshire can be seen whilst to the northwest, the Lakeland fells.

Forest of Bowland   Map 4 ref F5/6
8 miles SE of Lancaster

Designated an Area of Outstanding Natural Beauty in February
1964, this large scenic area is a veritable paradise for walkers and
country lovers that is dotted with picturesque villages. The 11th
largest of such designated areas, the Forest of Bowland is something of a misnomer, the term 'forest' is derived from the Latin 'foris'
which was formerly used to denote a royal hunting ground, an un-
enclosed tract of land, rather than a distinct wooded area. In fact,
even this description is not entirely correct as, in the 11th century,
the area was a chase - a private rather than a royal hunting ground.
Before 1066, Bowland was in the ownership of Earl Tostig of Northumbria, a brother of King Harold. Banished from his earldom, Tostig,

with the help of the King of Norway, attempted to regain his lands and both he and the Norwegian king were killed at Stamford Bridge, just weeks before the fateful Battle of Hastings.

Following the Norman Conquest, Bowland became part of the Honour of Clitheroe and the vast estates that belonged to the de Lacy family. In time, by marriage, they came into the hands of the Earls of Lancaster and, in 1399, when the then Duke of Lancaster ascended the throne as Henry IV, Bowland finally became one of nearly a hundred royal hunting forests.

The remains of a Roman road can be clearly seen traversing the land and many of the village's names in this area date back to the Saxon period. Perhaps the most celebrated of the many routes across Bowland is the minor road from Lancaster to Clitheroe which crosses **Abbeydale Moor** and the **Trough of Bowland** before descending into the lovely Hodder Valley around Dunsop Bridge. This is a popular route in the summer months, with most lay-bys and parking places filled as people pause to take in the breathtaking moorland views.

Slaidburn
15 miles SE of Lancaster on B6478

Map 3 ref G5

This pretty village, of stone cottages and cobbled pavements, lies in the heart of the Forest of Bowland. The village's focal point is the 13th century public house, **Hark to Bounty**, the name of which recalls the days when deer hunting was common in the area. The inn also contains an old courtroom, with its original oak furnishings, where, from around 1250, the Chief Court of Bowland, or Halmote, was held. The only courtroom between York and Lancaster, it was used by visiting justices from the 14th century onwards and is said to have been used by Oliver Cromwell when he was in the area.

From the village a network of beautiful, little used lanes radiate westwards up into the fell country with some of the best walking that Lancashire has to offer. One walk in particular, that offers solitude as well as an excellent taste of the Bowland landscape, is the that to the lonely valley of the River Whitendale, to the northwest of the village. To the northeast of Slaidburn lies Stocks Reservoir, another walker's destination.

Bolton by Bowland
21 miles SE of Lancaster off A59

Map 3 ref H6

Close to the River Ribble, this tranquil village with its ancient green, stone cross, and old stocks, lies on the southern edge of the forest area. The village church is home to the famous Pudsey tomb, with its engraved figure of Sir Ralph Pudsey in full armour alongside figures of his three wives and 25 children! Also here are many ornamental carvings.

Newton
Map 3 ref G6

15 miles SE of Lancaster on B6478

Little more than a hamlet, Newton lies on the main route between Clitheroe and Lancaster and so, in their time, both John Paslew, the last abbot of Whalley, and the Pendle witches passed through on their way to trial in Lancaster. Here, also, is a **Quaker Meeting House** that was founded in 1767: the associated Quaker school, where the 19th-century reformer John Bright was a pupil, has long since gone. Regarded with great suspicion by the Church of England, and by other nonconformists, because of their unorthodox views and their informality, the Quakers sought to settle in out of the way villages. Newton is typical of the places where they built their meeting houses and successfully lived according to their beliefs.

Dunsop Bridge
Map 2 ref F6

14 miles SE of Lancaster off B6478

Often known as the 'Gateway to the Trough of Bowland', Dunsop Bridge is, despite its remote location, the centre of the British Isles. The actual centre point, worked out by the Ordnance Survey, lies near Whitendale Hanging Stones and, to confirm the claim, the explorer Sir Ranolph Fiennes unveiled the commemorative plaque. British Telecommunications have also offered the village a unique honour by putting their 100,000th phone box here.

Whitewell
Map 2 ref F6

15 miles SE of Lancaster off B6478

Little more than a hamlet in the heart of the Forest of Bowland, Whitewell consists of a small church, built in the early 19th century on the site of a medieval chapel, and an inn, built on the site of the old manor house.

Just to the southeast lies **Browsholme Hall**, a Tudor mansion dating from 1507 that has the rare distinction of being occupied by the same family for all that time. From the 16th century onwards, the owners, the Parker family, were also bowbearers, or warders, of the Forest of Bowland - the king's agent and upholders of the law in the forest. Though much of the original Tudor house can still be seen, there have been many additions over the centuries, but it remains a homely building perhaps due to the continuous occupation by the same family and as a result of its remote location. The house is not open to the public.

Chipping

Map 2 ref F7

15 miles SE of Lancaster off B6243

This picturesque village overlooking the River Loud is now a conservation area and it is also home to a post office, built in 1668, which claims to be Britain's oldest shop. Very much at the heart of

Chipping Church

the local agricultural communities, the annual village show is one of the best in Lancashire and its very name comes from the old English for market place. In medieval times there were no less than five watermills along the banks of Chipping Beck and, later, one of the mills, Tweedies Mill, made ships' portholes which were used on the clipper ships bringing tea back from the east.

There are also a number of attractive inns here and one in particular, the Sun Inn, is also associated with a sad tale. Lizzy Dean, a serving wench at the inn, became engaged to a local man. On the morning of their wedding, on hearing the church bells ringing, Lizzie looked out of the window of her room at the inn and saw her bridegroom leaving the church with another bride on his arm. In deep despair, she hanged herself in the pub's attic and her last request was that her grave be dug in the path to the church so that her would-be groom had to walk over her grave each Sunday. This sad event took place in 1835 and Lizzie is still said to haunt the inn.

In the centre of Chipping stands **The Talbot Hotel**, a late 17th century inn that was originally built as a farmhouse. The Talbot's claim to fame is its resident ghost which, although it has never actually been seen, leaves a distinctive smell of lavender in its wake. The pub, managed by local man Len Rogerson and his wife Annie, has been refurbished with quality furnishings and decor but, to retain the olde worlde atmosphere, many of the building's original

The Talbot Hotel

features, such as the ceiling beams, remain. As well as serving an excellent pint of beer, The Talbot Hotel has a fine menu of tasty bar snacks and meals which are served both at lunchtime and in the evening (except Mondays). Behind the inn is a wonderful safe children's play area and also a large beer garden for adults. Football and rounders can also be played on the large playing field also found here. *The Talbot Hotel, Talbot Street, Chipping, Lancashire PR3 2QE Tel: 01995 61260*

CHAPTER TWO
The Ribble Valley

Cotton Martyrs, Corn Exchange, Preston

Chapter 2 - Area Covered

*For precise location of places please refer to the colour
maps found at the rear of the book.*

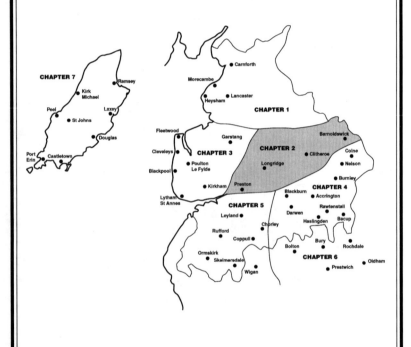

2
The Ribble Valley

Introduction

Flowing between the Forest of Bowland in the north and the hill country of Pendle in the south, the River Ribble cuts a pleasant and green course along a narrow valley. The **Ribble Way** middle-distance footpath follows the full 70 miles of the river, from its source in Yorkshire to the flat, tidal marshes of its estuary.

A beautiful, unspoilt yet small area, the Ribble Valley has long been a favourite with the people of Lancashire. Not only is it easily accessible but there are numerous gentle walks in the sheltered valley and a wealth of wildlife is supported by the lush countryside. It is also a place of pretty, untouched villages which the 20th century has left unchanged.

The central point of the valley is Clitheroe, a typical ancient Lancashire market town that is also home to one of the smallest Norman castles in the country. However, the Norman's were not the only invaders to built a fortification in the valley: further down stream lies Ribchester and the Roman fort of Bremetannacum. Up river from Clitheroe lies Sawley and another interesting ruin. The Cisterican monks of **Fountains Abbey** founded the religious house here in the 13th century and their influence, in the area of agriculture, can still be seen in the surrounding fields.

The valley is also home to two great houses. The first, Stonyhurst, was originally the home of the Shireburn family and it is now the world famous Roman Catholic public school. Whilst, on the outskirts of Preston, lies Salmesbury Hall, a wonderful 14th century house that is now a Mecca for antiques collectors.

River Ribble

Finally, at the mouth of the river lies Preston, the county's administrative centre and a town with more to offer than first appearances would suggest. Known to many as the home of the UK Snooker and World Indoor Bowls Championships, this ancient town also saw one of the key battles of the Civil War and it still continues the tradition of the Guild Celebrations. Dating back to medieval times and occurring once every 20 years, the week-long festival is well worth seeing.

Clitheroe

This old stone town, just south of the Forest of Bowland and in the valley of the River Ribble, has always been considered the forest's capital. It is also Lancashire's second oldest borough, to Wigan, receiving its first charter in 1147 and since then Clitheroe has served the surrounding villages of the Ribble Valley as their market town. Like Lancaster, it too is dominated by an 800 year-old **Castle** standing on a limestone crag high above the town. Now little more than a ruin, set in a small park, as visitors stand inside the keep, hidden voices relate the history of the castle, with suitable sound effects. During the Civil War, Clitheroe was a staunchly Royalist town but, fortunately, it and the castle survived the ravishes of the victorious Parliamentarians.

Clitheroe Castle and Museum

Found on a prominent limestone mound, close to the castle, is **Clitheroe Castle Museum**, home to many exhibits and displays which reflect the history and geology of the Ribble Valley area. Archaeological finds illustrate life in the valley from the earliest days of its inhabitation and in this section too can be seen the famous Hacking ferryboat now restored to its former glory. Closer to the present day is the recreation of an Edwardian kitchen, complete with its unique sound system that brings this turn of the century room to life.

As well as the local history displays the museum also has a fine collection relating to the geology of the area. Here, the appearance of the valley is explained in a series of unusual and interesting formats whilst the history of Salthill quarry is also explained. Now a nature reserve and place of special scientific interest, the quarry is famous for the fossils, which have been found there. Closed during January but open for the rest of the year, the museum not only offers a real insight into this delightful part of Lancashire but there is also a well stocked museum shop selling a wide range of books, postcards, and gifts. *Clitheroe Castle Museum, Castle Hill, Clitheroe, Lancashire, BB7 1BA Tel: 01200 424635*

On a neighbouring hill stands the parish **Church of St Mary Magdalen** which, though it was rebuilt by the Victorians, was founded in the 13th century. At this time too the town also had a school, however, the present **Royal Grammar School** was not established until 1554. The school's official charter, granted by Mary Tudor, was eventually found, in the vaults of a local solicitor's office, in 1990.

The town's narrow, winding streets are full of character and charm and, amidst the ancient buildings, is the rather incongruous **Civic Hall Cinema**. Built in the 1920s, this unspoilt monument to the golden days of the silver screen is still lined with plush velvet, has retained its grand piano that was used to accompany the silent films, and remains the town's cinema.

Just outside the town can be found **Edisford Picnic Area**, a popular place for family outings that stands on the site of a battle ground where the Scots fought the Normans. Also near to Clitheroe, at **Brungerley**, are a set of stepping stones across the river that are said to be haunted. Apparently the evil spirit living in the water drags a traveller to his watery death every seven years.

Just in the outskirts of the town, and only a few minutes walk from its castle, is **The Kings Arms Hotel**, a friendly pub that is

The Kings Arms Hotel

managed by Joy and Eric Jones, a local Lancashire couple. Originally built as a row of cottages in the late 17th century, the building became a public house around 200 years ago and, since then, The Kings Arms Hotel has been offering customers generous hospitality. Joy and Eric have continued the tradition and, as well as serving a good selection of real ales and the usual beers and lagers, they also have an extensive menu of home-cooked bar snacks and meals that are available at both lunchtime and in the evening. Entertaining customers also comes high on the list here and, as well as the separate games room, there is music each weekend evening and a large screen for showing sporting events. Children too are welcomed here, and they have their own purpose built play area. *The Kings Arms Hotel, 144 Bawdlands, Clitheroe, Lancashire BB7 2LA Tel: 01200 422450*

In the heart of Clitheroe, on King Street, lies **The Apricot Meringue**, a charming teashop that has a small Victorian frontage hiding a spacious interior. With three separate dining areas, one in a lovely conservatory at the rear of the property, intimacy is maintained whilst satisfying the many customers. For the past nine years partners, Terry Wild and Christopher Sharp, have been catering to the needs of shoppers and visitors to the town with a mouthwatering array of home-made, freshly cooked dishes.

The Apricot Meringue

Along with the more traditional hot and cold sandwiches, the menu also has a selection of delicious bistro-style dishes that cater for every taste and in particular to the hungrier client. The warm and friendly atmosphere makes this a superb and stylish place to stop. *The Apricot Meringue, 15 King Street, Clitheroe, Lancashire Tel: 01220 426933*

East of Clitheroe

Worston   *Map 3 ref G7*
1 mile NE of Clitheroe off A59

This tucked away village, down a lane off the main road, has remained unchanged over the years and can certainly be described as unspoilt. Keen-eyed visitors may even recognize the surrounding countryside as this was one of the locations used during the filming of *Whistle Down the Wind*. Behind the village inn, where the amusing and bizarre ritual of the village's Mock Corporation was revived in 1989, can still be seen the bull ring. Set into a stone, this was where the beast was tethered and baited with specially trained dogs in the belief that the 'sport' tenderized the meat.

Downham   *Map 3 ref H6*
3 miles NE of Clitheroe off A59

One of the most attractive villages in the area, Downham was purchased by the Assheton family in 1558 at the same time as they acquired Whalley Abbey. Beautifully maintained by the family, the present squire, Lord Clitheroe of Downham, still refuses to permit the skyline to be spoilt by television aerials, satellite dishes, and even dormer windows. The village phone box has also come under the influence of the family and it is not painted a distinctive pillar box red but grey, to tone in with the surroundings. The extent of the village's conservation has led to its use as a location for many films, the most famous being *Whistle Down the Wind*.

Rimington   *Map 3 ref H6*
5 miles NE of Clitheroe off A59

This rural village was the home of Francis Duckworth, the famous composer of hymn tunes including one named *Rimington*.

Gisburn   *Map 3 ref H6*
7 miles NE of Clitheroe on A59

Now within the boundaries of Lancashire, this village was once in Yorkshire and, as many locals would like to believe, it still is! One of the Ribble Valley's most pleasant and picturesque villages, its recent history is dominated by the Lister family who, from humble beginnings rose to become the Lords of Ribblesdale. Their house,

Downham Village

built in the early 17th century in **Gisburne Park**, is still standing though it is now a private hospital. Over the years, many people were given shelter by the family and, in 1648, Cromwell is said to have rested at the house whilst on his way to fight at Preston.

During the late 18th century, the family were rewarded for their loyalty to king and country, when they raised an army against Napoleon, by the creation of the title Lord of Ribblesdale in 1797. Coincidentally, the 4th and last Lord of Ribblesdale, who died in 1925 after having lost both his sons in World War I, shared the same name, Thomas, as the 1st Lord.

Standing on the main street in Gisburn, the distinctive **White Bull Hotel** is an attractive Grade II listed building that dates from the mid-19th century when the hotel provided hospitality to those travelling along one of Lancashire's main roads. Since April 1998, this family run inn has been owned and personally managed by sisters Kate Kirk and Moira Mortimer with the assistance of Ian, Moira's husband, Zilpah, her daughter, and her nephew, James.

Very much a country inn and restaurant, The White Bull Hotel offers its customers the chance to enjoy a drink and a meal in el-

The White Bull Hotel

egant surroundings and amid a friendly, relaxed atmosphere. Comfortably furnished and with stylish decoration inside, there is also plenty of space for customers to enjoy fresh air and the surrounding countryside in the inn's extensive rear gardens. Not only does the inn serve a range of real ales but the extensive menu of tasty, real food, bar snacks, and meals is sure to whet even the fussiest of appetites. With so much to offer already, Kate and Moira have made a great start in making The White Bull Hotel one of the best inns in the area. *The White Bull Hotel, Main Street, Gisburn, Lancashire BB7 4EH Tel: 01200 445575*

Paythorne   *Map 3 ref H5*
8 miles NE of Clitheroe off A682

Although the source of the River Ribble lies to the north in Yorkshire, near the famous Three Peaks of Whernside, Ingleborough, and Pen-y-ghent, this village is the first on its banks on this side of the county boundary. It also marks the end of the river's journey through the rugged limestone scenery of moorlands and the start of its picturesque course through a lush green valley.

The outstanding **Buck Inn**, in the heart of Paythorne, is a hidden gem that is well worth finding. This charming 18th century pub is not only attractive, both from the outside and inside, but it also is well known locally for the excellence of its cuisine, fine range of ales, and generous hospitality. Though Rachael and Ben have

The Buck Inn

been working here for sometime, they only became the owners in February 1998 but these superb hosts can certainly take much of the credit for the inn's fine reputation. As well as the excellent ales and beers from the bar, Ben, the chef of the partnership, has created a menu of tasty and imaginative dishes that are served both at lunchtime (except Mondays) and in the evening. The dining area, for which booking is essential at weekends, is dominated by a cardinal brick surround fireplace and the country theme which begins with the beamed ceiling and the table flowers is continued in the framed prints that hang on the walls. Just in case the delights of The Buck Inn itself are not enough, the pub occupies a scenic position with rolling countryside in every direction. *The Buck Inn, Kiln Lane, Paythorne, Lancashire BB7 4JD Tel: 01200 445488*

Sawley   *Map 3 ref H6*
3 miles E of Clitheroe off A59

At the centre of this historic village, easily missed as the main road by passes it, is **Sawley Abbey**, founded in the 13th century by the Cistercian monks of Fountains Abbey. As well as building their religious house, the monks had great influence over the whole of the surrounding area. Clearing their immediate surroundings, the monks cultivated the land and their ridge and furrow patterns can still be made out in the fields.

Although during the reigns Edward I and II, the abbots of Sawley were called to the House of Lords, none of the abbots were men of note except, perhaps, William Trafford, the last head of the community. With his colleague and neighbour, the last Abbot of Whalley, Trafford took part in the Pilgrimage of Grace in 1536 and, for his part in the failed uprising, he was taken prisoner. Tried for treason at Lancaster in 1537, Trafford, with others like him, was found guilty and executed.

During the 18th and 19th centuries, the land around the village, as elsewhere, was enclosed by drystone walls and, less so here, hedgerows. Today the landscape has changed little and it continues to support a wealth of wildlife.

West Bradford   Map 3 ref G6
1 mile N of Clitheroe off B6478

This tucked away village, just south of the Forest of Bowland, has a long history of rugged independence. Charming and attractive, a stream runs alongside the road through the bottom half of West Bradford and access to the houses bordering the beck is made by crossing a quaint stone bridge.

West of Clitheroe

Waddington   Map 3 ref G6
1 mile NW of Clitheroe on B6478

One of the area's best known villages, its attractive Coronation Gardens have appeared on many postcards and even on biscuit tin lids.

It was here, at Waddington Hall, that Henry VI lived for a year, in hiding, before being betrayed to the Yorkists. The king made his escaped, so the legend says, via a secret panel and staircase in the hall's dining room but he was quickly captured at Brungerley Bridge, down river near Clitheroe.

On a hill, just to the north of the village, lies **Bookers Farmhouse**, the home of Teresa and Philip Walsh. This delightfully located 250 year-old farm ceased being a working farm in the 1960s and, when Teresa and Philip bought the property in the early 1990s, it was derelict. After a complete renovation, the farmhouse has been restored very much to its former glory but with the addition of all the modern conveniences and comforts of the late 20th century.

From this charming home, the couple offer excellent bed and breakfast accommodation in a choice of two comfortable, en-suite rooms. Both are as pretty as a picture and, as well as the tremendous views across Lancashire's hill country, there is plenty of space and, in one of the rooms, a magnificent Victorian brass bedstead. The delicious home-cooked breakfast is served in the beautiful farmhouse-style kitchen and packed lunches are available to guests on

Bookers Farmhouse

request. This is a lovely place to stay that is ideally located in one of the most beautiful, yet undiscovered, parts of the country. *Bookers Farmhouse, Slaidburn Road, Waddington, near Clitheroe, Lancashire BB7 3JJ Tel: 01200 443893*

Found in the heart of the village, the **Waddington Arms** overlooks the village church as well as the stream, which runs through the centre of Waddington. The oldest parts of the building date back to the 15th century and the traditional appearance of the buildings exterior is carried through to the interior. Here, amid the

The Waddington Arms

oak-beamed ceilings and the open fires, visitors also get an insight into Andrew Warburton's (the pub's owner) enthusiasm for motor sport. Around the walls are numerous pictures and paintings of cars and motorbikes and also some fine drawings of famous racing drivers produced by local artists. During the summer, visitors can also take the opportunity to sit outside either at the front of the pub, on the charming patio area at the back, or in the beer garden.

As well as serving an excellent range of beers and ales, the Waddington Arms has a delicious menu of home-cooked dishes, which are served at both lunchtime and in the evening. There is also a house speciality, a local sausage that is made from a secret recipe dating back to 1880. With six comfortable en-suite bedrooms available for overnight guests, this is a superb place from which to explore the surrounding area. *The Waddington Arms, Waddington, near Clitheroe, Lancashire, BB7 3HP Tel: 01200 423262*

Great Mitton
Map 3 ref G7

3 miles SW of Clitheroe on B6246

Standing opposite the Three Fishes Hotel, which takes its name from the three fishes on the Whalley Abbey coat of arms, is the attractive **All Hallows' Church**. Housing some of the finest relics to be seen in any British church, this is most certainly worth a visit. Built in around 1270, though undoubtedly there was a wooden Saxon structure hereabouts, little has been done to the building since although a tower was added in 1438 and the pews are Jacobean. However, it is the **Shireburn Chapel** that draws most visitors to the church. Added in the mid-15th century by the Shireburn family of Stonyhurst they claimed to be the direct descendants of the first rector, Ralph the Red of Mytton. Containing memorials to family members, perhaps the chapel's most impressive feature is the fine alabaster tomb of Sir Richard Shireburn and his wife Maude.

Confirmation that a settlement existed here before the days of the land ownership by the abbey comes with the name of the village itself. Mitton is derived from the Saxon word 'mythe' which means a farm at the junction of two rivers - perfectly describing the location as, close by, the River Hodder feeds into the River Ribble.

Hurst Green
Map 2 ref F7

5 miles SW of Clitheroe on B6243

This pretty village, of stone-built cottages nestling in the Ribble Valley, is best known for its nearby public school. **Stonyhurst College**, the world famous Roman Catholic school, began life as the residence of the local lords of the manor. The present building, begun in around 1523, was the work of Hugh Shireburn although additions were made in 1592 by Sir Richard Shireburn. An ambitious man, Sir Richard served the Tudor monarchy and, as well as being the Chief Forester of Bowland, he was also one of Henry VIII's commissioners studying the state of the monasteries and he was an eager participant in the suppression of Whalley Abbey. Though the family took on the new Protestant religion under Elizabeth I, it was with little spirit and in a short time the Shireburn family, like many other Lancashire families, returned to their Catholic faith. It seems strange then that Cromwell, on his way to and from the Battle of Preston, should take shelter at Stonyhurst and rumour has it that the ardent Puritan slept with a pistol at his side and his guards around him.

In 1794, after the house had been left for some considerable time and had fallen into a state of disrepair, the owner, Thomas Weld, offered the property to the Jesuits who had set up an English Catholic School in Flanders. Unwelcome in France following the revolution, the Jesuits gladly accepted and, after restoring the original building, they extended it during the 19th century. Their finest addition must be the replica of King's College in Cambridge: ***St Peter's Church*** was built in 1835 and it includes many treasures including a 7th century copy of St John's Gospel and a cope of Henry II that was used by Henry VIII at the battle of the Field of the Cloth of Gold. One of the college's most famous sons is Sir Arthur Conan Doyle, the creator of Sherlock Holmes.

Ribchester   Map 2 ref F8
7 miles SW of Clitheroe on B5269

Situated on the banks of the River Ribble, the village is famous for its ***Roman Fort***, Bremetannacum, on the northern river bank. It was the Roman governor, Gnaeus Julius Agricola, in AD 79, who first established a fort here at the junction of the two important roads between Manchester and Carlisle, and York and the west coast. Although little of the fort's walls remain, the granary or storehouse, with its hypocaust (underfloor heating), has been excavated and has revealed some interesting coins, pottery, sculptures, and inscriptions.

The fort's ***Roman Museum*** is designed to transport visitors back to the days of the Roman occupation and it offers an excellent insight into those times. Unfortunately, the finest artefact found on the site, an ornate helmet, is not on display here (though they do have a replica) but it can be seen in the British Museum in London.

Back in the village proper, the discovery of some pre-Norman Conquest crosses in and around **St Wilfrid's Church** would suggest that this 13th century building occupies the site of a Saxon church. The church is named after the first Bishop of Ripon, who in the 7th century took a prominent role in the Synod of Whitby, and this would seem to confirm the earlier buildings existence in the absence of any direct evidence.

A great place for tourists during the summer months, Ribchester not only has these two sights to offer but also several excellent pubs, restaurant, and cafés which provide much needed refreshment. Finally, Ribchester has one further attraction, the **Museum of Childhood** that is housed in the village's old Co-op building. The collection is diverse and goes back to the days of the Victorian music hall, with many of the models still in working order.

Dating back to the 17th century, the building that is home to **Miles House Farm Restaurant** was originally a farmhouse, the kitchen was the old dairy, and the restaurant itself is housed in the barn where older villagers can still remember corn being threshed. A restaurant for some 30 years, Miles House is named after a local ferryman who worked the nearby River Ribble, and, today, it is owned and run by Christine Marshall. A wonderful place to find for those who enjoy their food, the restaurant is open during the day from Wednesday to Sunday and in the evening from Wednesday to Saturday. Such is the popularity of Miles House Farm Restaurant that booking is necessary at all times.

For lunch the menu concentrates on traditional English cuisine, such as roast joints and steak and kidney pie, whilst, in the evening, the extensive menu is one of classical French dishes. During the summer, the cream teas, served outside if the weather is fine, are

Miles House Farm Restaurant

also very popular. All the dishes are home-cooked by Christine, an excellent and experienced chef who delights in creating delicious meals from local, fresh ingredients.

However, Miles House Farm Restaurant has more to offer customers than fine food and wine as there are also three comfortable bed and breakfast rooms available in the main farmhouse. The building is set within an acre of wonderful designated wildlife garden. *Miles House Farm Restaurant, Blackburn Road, Dutton, Nr Ribchester, Lancashire PR3 3ZQ Tel & Fax: 01254 878204*

Stydd   Map 2 ref F8
7 miles W of Clitheroe off B6245

Just to the north of Ribchester lies the small hamlet of Stydd. All that remains of the monastery founded here by the Knights Hospitallers of St John of Jerusalem is the Norman **Chapel** which contains effigies of some of the knights. A crusading and military order established in 1113, the Knights Hospitallers provided help and assistance to pilgrims travelling to the Holy Land. Their commandery, as their religious houses were called, at Stydd was dissolved by the mid-14th century and, although at one time there were over 50 of their small monasteries in the country, only 15 survived to the 1530s.

Longridge   Map 2 ref E7
10 miles W of Clitheroe on B6243

The village lies at the foot of **Longridge Fell** from which there are some superb views northwards over the Loud valley to Chipping: to the south the land drops away towards the River Ribble. For many years this area was an important source of building stone and several of Preston's civic buildings and the docks at Liverpool were constructed with Longridge stone.

Goosnargh   Map 2 ref E7
12 miles W of Clitheroe on B5269

Just to the west of the village lies **Chingle Hall**, a small moated manor house that was built in 1260 by Adam de Singleton. A Catholic family, the Singletons are said to have a chapel with three priest hides and, so the story goes, Cromwell once climbed down one of the hall's chimneys to spy on the Royalists below. As well as being the birthplace of St John Wall, one of the last priests to die for his faith, in 1620, it is well known as one of the most haunted houses in Britain and, as such, the hall has featured on countless television and radio programmes.

Grimsargh
Map 2 ref E8

11 miles W of Clitheroe on B6243

As well as having one of the largest village greens in Lancashire, covering some 12 acres, Grimsargh is also home to **Tun Brook Wood**. Following the line of the brook until it meets the River Ribble, this is thought to be one of the largest areas of deciduous woodland in the country.

Salmesbury
Map 2 ref E8

12 miles W of Clitheroe on A59

To the east of the village, close to the busy main road, lies **Salmesbury Hall**, built by the Southworth family. The hall seen today it actually the second house they built as their original hall was burned to the ground by Robert the Bruce in the early 14th century. Thinking that the original position, close to a crossing of the River Ribble was too vulnerable to attack, the family built their subsequent home in what was then an isolated location.

More peaceful times followed and the hall, surrounded by a moat and with a drawbridge, was a reflection of the family's wealth. A staunchly Catholic family, their 15th century chapel contains a mullioned Gothic window that was rescued from Whalley Abbey after the Dissolution in the 1530s. However, it was the loyalty to their faith that finally saw the demise of the Southworth family. Their continued practice of Catholicism saw Sir John Southworth imprisoned in Manchester in the late 16th century and, by the time of his death a few years later, the family, having kept their faith, had seen their fortune dwindle away.

The hall was sold to the Braddyll family who, having a house near Ulverston, simple stripped Salmesbury Hall of its assets. Some how the hall survived though, by the 1870s it was in a shocking state of repair. First, Joseph Harrison stepped in and began a successful restoration programme, to the point where he was able to entertain the likes of Charles Dickens. However, the building work took all his money and, facing ruin, Harrison committed suicide. Once more in need of rescue, the hall was saved by the Salmesbury Hall Trust, a group who are still managing the property today.

The hall's unusual history is only equalled by the unconventional manner in which it, quite literally, earns its keep. With no assets left, after being stripped by the Braddylls, the hall is once again full of antiques but these are all for sale. As salerooms go, this has to be one of the most atmospheric.

Preston   *Map 2 ref E8*
15 miles W of Clitheroe on A59

Lancaster may have the distinction of being the county town, but
Preston is Lancashire's administrative centre and its location makes
it an excellent place from which to explore the whole region. Despite first appearances, Preston is a town of ancient history and it is
strategically positioned on the highest navigable point of the River
Ribble. However, the port activity has declined, the dockland area,
now called **Riversway**, has become an area of regeneration, and the
marina caters now for pleasure craft, yachts, and windsurfers.

Though the town has both a Roman and a medieval past nothing
of this is visible today. However, the lasting legacy of those days is
reflected in the famous Guilds Celebrations which have been taking place every 20 years since 1500. The Royal Charter establishing
the rights to hold a Guild Merchant was granted by Henry II in
1179. These medieval guilds were unions of tradesmen who came
together in the pursuit of fair dealing and with the intention of pre-
venting cheats from offering a second rate service. Each guild
operated from what amounted to their own weights and measures
office, the guild hall. As the guilds grew they also became insurance
companies, looking after any member who was taken ill and unable
to work. In order to ensure the high standards within a given trade
were maintained the apprentice system was started and any member found to be cheating or offering substandard workmanship was
expelled from the guild. The last Guild Celebration took place in
1992 and, already, preparations are being made for the next.

Preston also featured in the Domesday Book, though, at that
time it was known as Priest-town and, in the 1260s, the Greyfriars
settled here. The Catholic traditions of Preston continued, as they
did elsewhere in the county, and this has, along with the associated
loyalty to the crown, had a great part to play in the town's history.
During the Civil War, it was the Battle of Preston, in 1648, which
confirmed the eventual defeat of the supporters of Charles I and,
later, at the time of the 1745 Jacobite rebellion, Preston played host
to Prince Charles Edward.

The many public buildings of Preston all reflect the prosperity of
the town during the Victorian age. This wealth was built upon the
textile industry helped by the general location of the town: midway
between London and Glasgow, on a major railway route, and with
the docks. Though the town's prosperity was built on cotton, textiles were not new to Preston as linen had been produced here from
as far back as Tudor times. Preston was also the place where, in

1768, the single most important machine of the textile industry was invented: Richard Arkwright's water-frame cotton spinning machine. Almost overnight, the cottage industries of spinning and handloom weaving were moved from the workers' homes into factories and the entrepreneurs of Preston were quicker than most to catch on. One gentleman in particular, John Horrocks, saw the potential of combining the spinning and weaving operations under the same roof and so he was able to take raw cotton in and produce the finished article on delivery. His firm became the largest of its kind in the world, further adding to the town's prosperity, but it did not do Horrocks himself much good as, by the age of 36, he was dead.

Although the great days of the textile industry are long gone in Preston, as elsewhere in Britain, the cotton workers of the town are remembered in a statue which stands outside the old **Corn Exchange**.

Looking at the town now it is hard to imagine those hectic days and may be even hard to believe that, when the docks were com-

Cotton Martyrs, Corn Exchange

pleted here in 1892, Preston was the second largest container handling port in Britain. In 1900, 1,285 vessels carrying nearly half a million tons of cargo entered and left the port. Unfortunately, the battle of keeping the channel open and free of silt became too expensive, particularly as trade was lost to other, non-tidal ports, and the docks eventually closed.

One of the best places to start any exploration of the town is the *Harris Museum and Art Gallery*. Housed in a magnificent neoclassical building which dominates the Market Square, the museum and art gallery were opened in 1893. Funded by a successful local businessman and reminiscent of the British Museum, as well as the fine collection of paintings and watercolours by major 19th century British artists, there is an excellent exhibition of the story of Preston. The two other museums in the town are regimental. Housed in the former county court building, and with limited opening, the *County and Regimental Museum*, which is guarded by a giant Howitzer gun, has galleries dedicated to three regiments: the 14th/20th Kings Hussars, the Duke of Lancaster's Own Yeomanry, and the Queen's Lancashire Regiment. There is also an interesting and very informative display on the history of Lancashire. The Fulwood Barracks, which were built in 1848 of Longridge stone, are also home to the *Loyal Regiment (North Lancashire) Museum*. With a rich history that covers many campaigns, the exhibits here are numerous and include the famous silver mounted Maida Tortoise, items connected with General Wolfe, souvenirs from the Crimea War, and artefacts from the Defence of Kimberley, the diamond town in South Africa which the 1st Battalion the Loyals defended single-handedly.

Preston's *Guild Hall*, built in 1972 to celebrate that year's Guild, is known, or at least its interior, to many snooker and bowls fans as it is the venue for the UK Snooker and the World Indoor Bowls Championships. Another building, less well-known but still a distinctive landmark is *Preston Prison*. Built in 1789, it replaced the town's first House of Correction. In an interesting move in providing the inmates with work, during the 19th century, looms were installed in the prison and the prisoners were paid for their labour. Industrial unrest in the area soon followed and, in 1837, it was only the threat of a cannon which saved the prison from invasion by an angry mob intent on destroying the machines. Although the prison was closed in 1931, it re-opened in 1948 and remains so.

As might be expected for a town on the banks of a river, there are many bridges but two crossings are particularly worthy of note. *Penwortham Old Bridge* is perhaps the most attractive in Lancashire; slightly hump-backed and built of a mixture of stone. Constructed chiefly of buff gritstone and pink sandstone in 1756, it replaced a bridge that had collapsed and, by 1912, its use by motor cars and heavy carts was prohibited. For over 150 years, the bridge was the lowest crossing of the River Ribble. By contrast, the ***Ribble Viaduct*** is a completely different structure. One of the oldest works of railway engineering in the area and a construction of great elegance and dignity, it was built in 1838 and brought the railway from Wigan to the centre of Preston.

CHAPTER THREE
The Fylde

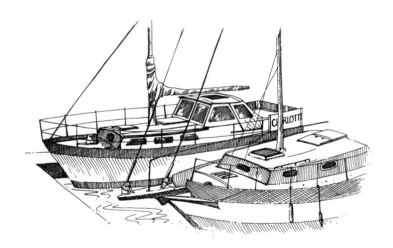

Fleetwood Harbour

Chapter 3 - Area Covered

For precise location of places please refer to the colour maps found at the rear of the book.

3
The Fylde

Introduction

This historic area of coastal Lancashire is known to many as the home of Blackpool: the brash, seaside resort that has been entertaining holidaymakers for generations. To the south lies another resort, Lytham St Anne's, which is not only somewhat more genteel but also the home of one of the country's most well known golf courses and host to the British Open Championships. Both places grew up as a result of the expansion of the railway system in the Victorian age, when they were popular destinations for the mill workers of Lancashire and Yorkshire.

However, the Fylde is also an ancient region that was known to both the Saxons and the Romans. To the north of this region, around the Wyre estuary, the salt marshes have been exploited for over 2,000 years and the process continues at the large ICI plant. Fishing and shipping too have been important sources of revenue here. Fleetwood is still a port though smaller than it was whilst, surprisingly though it might seem today, Lytham was also an important port along the Ribble Estuary.

Inland, the fertile, flat plain has been farmed for many centuries and, with few major roads, the quiet rural communities lie undisturbed and little changed by the 20th century. A haven for wildlife, and particularly birds and plants, the two estuaries, of the Ribble and the Wyre, provide habitats that abound with rare and endangered species of plants and birds. A relatively undiscovered region, the Fylde has much more to offer than a white knuckle ride and candy floss and is well worth taking the time to explore.

Blackpool

Probably Britain's liveliest and most popular resort, certainly it is a place that everyone in the country has heard of even if they do not know where it is. Blackpool, like it or loath it, is definitely an experience. A typical British resort, with piers, funfairs, gardens, amusement arcades, and a promenade, although they all appear much bigger here, not even the rather wet northwest coast weather is able to dampen the spirits of the many who flock here for their two weeks holiday or just for a day out by the sea.

It is hard to believe that, just over 150 years ago, Blackpool was little more than a fishing village among the sand dunes of the Fylde coast. At that time, travel to and from the village involved considerable discomfort, taking a day from Manchester and two days from York. However, it was the arrival of the great Victorian railway companies that put Blackpool well and truly on the map by laying the railway lines right to the coast and building the grand stations - the town had three. The quiet fishing village was quickly transformed into a vibrant resort as day-trippers from the mill towns of Lancashire and Yorkshire took advantage of the cheap excursion rail fares.

It was the late 19th century which saw the building of many of the resort's now famous attractions. At that time it was estimated that Blackpool's 7,000 dwellings could accommodate 250,000 holidaymakers in addition to a permanent population of 35,000. As these visitors would also need entertainments and amusements the town's development began in earnest. In 1889, the original Opera House was built in the Winter Gardens complex and two years later a start was made on the world famous *Tower*. Completed in 1894, the world famous tower, modelled on the Eiffel Tower in Paris, stands some 518 feet high and for over 100 years it has been a well-known landmark, visible from many miles away. The centenary celebrations were numerous and extravagant and included painting the tower gold! However, unlike its French counterpart, the tower is not just a skeletal building but is also home to the almost as famous *Tower Ballroom*. Elegant and a much loved institution, tea dances are still a regular feature here and it was, for many years, the venue for the BBC *Come Dancing* competition

The *North Pier,* designed by Eugenius Birch, was opened at the beginning of the 1863 season. It soon became the place to promenade and it is now a listed building. The *Pleasure Beach*, which boasts its own railway station, is an attraction that continues to be

extended and improved. Home to the tallest, fastest, and possibly
the most expensive roller coaster ride in the world, some of its delights are not for the fainthearted.

Close to the Pleasure Beach is a relatively new attraction that
the British weather cannot spoil. *The Sandcastle* provides all-
weather fun in a water environment, with waves, waterslides, and
flumes in a tropical indoor setting. Further down the Golden Mile,
The Sea Life Centre, again reflecting the water theme, proves popular with all ages and gives visitors a close-up view of the creatures
of the underworld.

Despite its reputation as a brash and lively resort, Blackpool
also has its quiet, secluded corners where visitors can escape the
hustle of the crowds. There are seven miles of sea front, from the
North Shore down as far as Squire's Gate and Lytham, where the
pace of life is gentler and the beaches are quieter. Blackpool *Tram-
ways* have provided a most enjoyable way of exploring these less
busy sides the town and it environs for many years. And, it should
also be remembered that the world's first electric street tram system opened here in 1885. The route was extended along the Lytham
road in 1895 and later connecting with other routes in nearby Lytham
and St Anne's. However bus services, which put paid to many town's
tram routes, left by the 1960s Blackpool's tram system as the only
commercial route in the country.

Still a popular means of transport here today, many of the tram-
cars dates from the 1930s or 1950s and the managing company has
a special selection of vintage cars which they run on special occasions. One of these occasions is the now annual *Illuminations*
which, following a ceremonial lighting much like that of the Christ-
mas lights in London, is a splendid end to the season. An eagerly
awaited free show, running the full length of the promenade, the
lights have, over the years, provided many spectacular shows and
incorporated many themes.

Once a village in its own right, *Marton* is now a smart suburb of
Blackpool and also the home of *The Shovels* public house. Built in
the 1950s, on the site of the original Shovels inn, the pub has recently been refurbished and, though it has a modern, open plan, the
furnishings and decorations are very yesteryear. The hospitality
offered by landlord Stephen and his wife Helen is also olde worlde
and The Shovels is once more becoming a place to which people
flock for excellent beer, food, and a warm and friendly atmosphere.
As well as serving a range of well-kept real ales, such as Director's
and Theakston's, the menu, which is served all day, includes more

The Shovels

adventurous dishes using kangaroo, crocodile, and ostrich. Mark, the chef, is Australian, which would explain the more unusual nature of some of his creations, but he is also becoming well known and well recommended for his culinary skills. As well as the charming conservatory restaurant, customers can take their meal, less formally, anywhere in the rest of this comfortable inn. The Shovels is open all day, every day, and its outstanding exterior makes it hard to miss. *The Shovels, 260 Common Edge Road, Marton, Blackpool, Lancashire FY4 5DA Tel: 01253 762702 Fax: 01253 699635*

Situated at **Peel**, just a short drive from the centre of Blackpool, **Under Hill Farm Camp Site** is an established park that has been owned and run by Marjorie and Tom Pickervance for many years. Standing in peaceful and tranquil surroundings within a 100 acre dairy farm, but away from the actual farming business, the site has hard and soft pitches for touring caravans and it is also popular with campers who pitch under canvas. Open throughout the season, from Easter to the end of the Blackpool's illuminations, Under Hill Farm has all the modern facilities expected by today's campers and it is also the ideal place for children. Dogs too are welcome,

Under Hill Farm Camp Site

though they must be kept on a lead. Friendly and relaxed, the site also offers glorious views of the Fylde countryside and is ideally placed for many of Lancashire's attractions. *Under Hill Farm Camp Site, Preston New Road, Peel, Blackpool, Lancashire FY4 5JS Tel: 01253 763107*

North of Blackpool

Thornton   *Map 1 ref B7*
5 miles N of Blackpool on B5268

Situated in the west bank of the Wyre estuary, this small town is dominated by **Marsh Mill**, which stands over 100 feet high and was constructed in 1794. The grinding of corn ceased here soon after World War I but the building has been restored and it is now a tourist attraction.

At this point the Wyre estuary is wide and provides shelter for shipping, an advantage that was utilised by both the Romans and the Scandinavians. They both, also, took advantage of the salt deposits here and, today, the large ICI plant is still extracting salt. The **Wyre Estuary Country Park**, taking the whole estuary from Fleetwood up river as far as Shard Bridge, is an excellent place from which to discover the area. An initial stop at the Wyreside Ecology Centre, which provides all manner of information about the estuary, is a sensible starting point. From here a number of footpaths take in many of the places along the river as well as leading visitors through important areas of salt marsh which contain a wide range of plants, insects, and birds.

Cleveleys   *Map 1 ref B7*
5 miles N of Blackpool on A584

This popular seaside resort is less boisterous than its neighbour to the south and it is altogether more attractive - architecturally. This is hardly surprising as the town began to grow after an architectural competition, organised in 1906, in which Sir Edwin Lutyens, the designer of modern Whitehall, London, was involved.

Fleetwood   *Map 1 ref B6*
8 miles N of Blackpool on A587

This fishing town, on the northern tip of the Fylde coast, is a planned town founded in the early 19th century around the Wyre deepwater port. Based on a form street pattern radiating from the Mount, the development was undertaken by the then landowner, Sir Peter

Hesketh-Fleetwood, who wished to create a new holiday resort for working class people from the industrial mill towns of east Lancashire. Prior to the commencement of the building work in 1836, this had been a small settlement of a few fishermen's cottage. The opening of the railway extension from Preston to Fleetwood was a key player in the town's development and the North Euston Hotel, which opened in 1842, reflects those railway links. Queen Victoria used Fleetwood as she travelled to Scotland for her annual holiday. However, this was all before the railway companies managed to lay a railway over Shap fell in Cumbria in 1847 and thus provide a direct rail link to Scotland.

The town's **Museum**, overlooking the River Wyre, illustrates the town's links with the fishing industry which suffered greatly from the Icelandic cod wars. However, Fleetwood's real claim to fame is the **Fisherman's Friend** - a staggeringly successful lozenge that was used by fishermen to relieve sore throats and bronchial trouble caused by the freezing conditions found in the northern Atlantic waters. In 1865, James Lofthouse, a chemist in the town, combined the ingredients of liquorice, capsicum, eucalyptus, and methanol, into a liquid for the town's fishermen but, as the seas were invariably rough, the bottles were broken before the men could benefit from the mixture. So Lofthouse, undefeated, combined the same ingredients into a lozenge that proved much more practical on board ship and, in a very short space of time his shop was inundated with

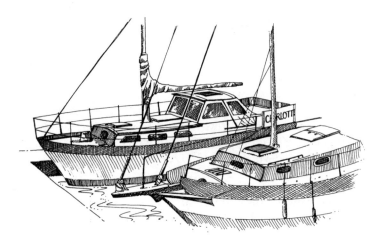

Fleetwood Harbour

customers. Today, Fishermen's Friends, which remain unchanged from the original recipe, are still produced by the same family business and their sales are now worldwide.

Rossall Point   Map 1 ref B6
7 miles N of Blackpool off A587
Situated at the northern tip of the Fylde coast, this was where the Hesketh-Fleetwood family, the force behind the creation of Fleetwood, had their home. Their impressive mansion is still standing and is now part of Rossall School.

Preesall   Map 1 ref C6
8 miles N of Blackpool on B5270
The village's original name, Pressoude, as it was mentioned in the Domesday Book, is thought to mean a salt farm near the sea and certainly in 1872 rock salt deposits were discovered beneath the village. From then on, for around 30 years, Preesall became a centre for salt mining and, in 1883, the Fleetwood Salt Company was established to develop the field. The bulk of the salt was extracted in the form of brine and, by the end of 1891, there was a reliable pipeline pumping the salt under the River Wyre to Fleetwood.

However, as much of the salt was extracted from underneath the expanding village, subsidence soon became a problem and, in 1923, this led to the opening up of a huge pit, known locally as 'Bottomless' to the west of the village.

Knott End-on-Sea   Map 1 ref C6
8 miles N of Blackpool on B5270
This small coastal resort, on the River Wyre estuary, grew into a substantial fishing settlement in the 17th and 18th centuries. It was also a pilot base for the upstream ports of Wardleys and Skippool and later developed into a ferry port. However, today, its broad flat sands and bracing sea air, along with the decline in the fishing industry, have turned the town into a small, quiet holiday resort that is also favoured by those who have retired.

Looking out to sea, at low tide, a rocky outcrop can be seen which, some historians have suggested, is the remains of the masonry of a Roman port. Whether this is the port that, in the 2nd century Ptolomy marked on a map as ***Portus Setantiorum***, is certainly in doubt but it is undeniable that such a building existed as the Romans were planning an invasion of Ireland from this stretch of coast.

Standing on the esplanade, the well recommended ***Farm Kitchen Café*** overlooks Morecambe Bay and has panoramic views over to the Cumbrian towns of Cartmel, Grange-over-Sands, and Silverdale. Owned and personally run by Lorna and Manolo Rey, this popular café serves a wide range of home-cooked dishes that has people coming from far and wide to visit. Open all year round, but closed on Wednesdays, it is not only the excellent food that draws people to the café but the lovely atmosphere of the place that this charming couple have created. With plenty of comfortable seating to satisfy customers the café walls display prints from local artists, including

The Farm Kitchen Café

Lancashireman Tom Riley, that are also for sale - the ideal way to remember a visit to this excellent café. *The Farm Kitchen Café, 3-5 The Esplanade, Knott End-on-Sea, Lancashire FY6 0AD Tel: 01253 811651*

Situated right on the shoreline, **The Bourne Arms Hotel** looks out across the River Wyre estuary to Fleetwood. Built in the mid-19th century by the local landowning family, the Bournes, the premises were sold in 1901 to a local brewery and given a licence. It was here, years later, that the inn's present owners first met as teenagers when they were both working here. Eileen and Peter Dobby bought the pub in 1995 and, together, they have turned it into a popular place that not only provides its many customers with a fine range of real ales but also a delicious menu of mouthwatering dishes. As pretty as a picture both inside and out, there is a charming outdoor patio area that is ideal in fine weather as well as an indoor conservatory. Many of the buildings original features still remain. As well as the ceiling beams and leaded windows, this distinctive black and white painted building is home to a splendid six

The Bourne Arms Hotel

foot model of the Kingston Diamond trawler. *The Bourne Arms Hotel, Bourne May Road, Knott End-on-Sea, Lancashire FY6 0AB Tel: 01253 810256*

Pilling
Map 1 ref C6
10 miles N of Blackpool off A588

This quiet scattered village, on the edge of rich, fertile marshland, was, for many years, linked to the market town of Garstang by a little, winding, single-track railway known affectionately as the 'Pilling Pig'.

Said to be the second largest village in Britain, Pilling is steeped in history. The Olde Ship Inn, for example, was built in 1782 by George Dickson, a slave trader. Now a listed building, the inn is reputed to be haunted by a lady dressed in Georgian attire, wandering around with a pale and worried look on her face.

Garstang
Map 1 ref D6
12 miles N of Blackpool on A6

This is an ancient, picturesque town whose market dates back to the time of Edward II, who granted the monks the right to hold the market. Thursday is still market day and both the High Street and the Market Hall become a hive of activity. As the town is situated close to a ford over the River Wyre, visitors will not be surprised to learn that the town dates back to the 6th century when a Saxon, named Garri, made his base here. The town's name comes from the Old Scandinavian words of 'geirr' meaning spear and 'stong' meaning pole.

The town is also home to an excellent **Discovery Centre** which deals with a variety of aspects of the region, including the history of the nearby Forest of Bowland and the natural history of the surrounding countryside.

Just to the east of the town, on the top of a grassy knoll, are the remains of **Greenhalgh Castle**, built in 1490 by Thomas Stanley, the first Earl of Derby. Severely damaged in a siege against Cromwell in 1645-46, the castle is reputed to be one of the last strongholds in Lancashire to have held out.

A little to the north, on the A6, are the remains of a stone-built **Toll House** which probably dates from the 1820s when parts of the turnpike from Garstang to Lancaster were realigned. Although a ruin, the toll house is more than usually interesting as the posts for the toll gates can still be seen on either side of the road. This stretch of road is also home to some of the finest **Turnpike Milestones** in the county. To the south of Garstang, they are round-faced stones with cursive lettering dating from the 1750s and, to the north, the stones are triangular, with Roman lettering, and date from the time of the turnpike's realignment in the early 19th century.

The Royal Oak Hotel, in the centre of Garstang, has been managed by the Hewitson family since 1959; first by Betty and James and now by Michael and Lorraine. Said to date from 1480, the building was originally a farmhouse that brewed its own beer but, in the mid-17th century, it became a well-known coaching inn on the main route between London and Edinburgh. Recently refurbished to a high standard, this charming inn has a cosy lounge bar and a snug

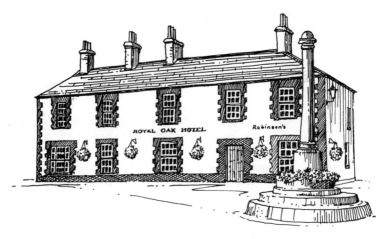

The Royal Oak Hotel

bar, complete with oak panelling and old stained glass where tasty bar snacks and meals are available as well as an range of real ales. Those wishing to enjoy their refreshments outside can also take advantage of the secluded beer garden. The dining room is equally attractive and traditional in looks and this popular restaurant is the ideal place for a delicious meal out. However, this is not all that the Royal Oak Hotel has to offer as there are also 10 comfortable en-suite guest bedrooms where visitors can be assured of a superb night's rest in these relaxing surroundings. *The Royal Oak Hotel, Market Place, Garstang, Lancashire PR3 1ZA Tel: 01995 603318 Fax: 01995 606529*

Hambleton
Map 1 ref C7
6 miles NE of Blackpool on A588

A centre for ship building in medieval times, Hambleton is now a quiet village on the banks of the River Wyre from which radiate a network of narrow lanes that wind through the charming north Fylde countryside.

The village also stands on one of the narrowest parts of the river and there was certainly a ford in Roman times, as relics have been found here. However, it is probable that the ford goes back even further, to the Iron Age, around 500 BC. On the site of the ford now stands the 325-yard **Shard Bridge**, built in 1864 and which still operates as a toll bridge.

Stalmine
Map 1 ref C6
7 miles NE of Blackpool on A588

Lying to the north of the village near Stalmine and close to an area of drained mossland, is Moor End Farm, home of **Minefleet Farm Shop** and **The Old Trough Organic Tearooms**. The farm has

**Minefleet Farm Shop and Old Trough
Organic Tearooms**

been a family-run pig farm for over 60 years and the present owners, Barbara and Bevan Ridehalgh keep a herd of rare and mixed breed pigs selected for the flavour of the pork. In addition, they have created a wonderful attraction that the whole family will enjoy. The shop and tearooms can be found in converted buildings around a farmyard typical of those once common in the area. The yard is dominated by a barn of Tudor origin and there are uninterrupted views from it across the countryside as far as the hills of the Trough of Bowland.

The Old Trough Tearooms offer a full range of home-cooked meals and snacks that are mainly organic and, at least, additive-free. The couple's aim of serving excellent food in pleasant surroundings has certainly been realised and the needs of vegetarians have not been forgotten. Naturally, the shop sells Minefleet pure pork, so called because it comes from pigs which have not had antibiotics and synthetic growth-promoters in their feed. Customers may buy anything from sausages and chops to half a pig for the freezer.

Not surprisingly, the Minefleet Farm Shop also sells organic products including food for people with special dietary needs, such as dairy-free. The selection of organic products is exceptionally wide-ranging, from vegetables and fruit, through to cereals, bread, and jams, to teas and coffees, not forgetting the ice-cream which is sure to please the palate. Visitors to the shop and tearooms also have the opportunity to see a variety of animals and poultry, including pigs, ponies, goats, and geese. In spring 1993, Barbara and Bevan created two woods, which involved the planting of 2,500 mixed species of trees, and not only do they now provide pleasant walks, they are also a haven for wildlife. *Minefleet Farm Shop and The Old Trough Organic Tearooms, Moor End Farm, Back Lane, Stalmine, Poulton-le-Fylde, Lancashire FY6 0LN Tel: 01253 700229*

East of Blackpool

Poulton-le-Fylde   *Map 1 ref C7*
4 miles E of Blackpool on A586

This is one of the oldest towns in the ancient area known as Amounderness. The Romans were known to have been in the area and it was probably their handiwork that constructed the **Danes Pad**, an ancient trackway. The town developed as a commercial centre for the surrounding agricultural communities and its Market Place remains its focal point. In 1732, a great fire, started by sparks from the torches of a funeral procession, destroyed most of the thatched cottages that surrounded the market square in those days and a nationwide appeal was launched to help meet the rebuilding costs. Consequently, little of old Poulton can be seen in the centre of the town.

The present **Church of St Chad** dates from the early 17th century, though the majority of the building is Georgian, and it stands on the site of the original Norman church. Inside, which is true Georgian, there is a splendid staircase, unusual for a church, leading up to the gallery which runs around three sides of the building. As Poulton was a key town in the area for centuries, it is not surprising that there are several magnificent memorials to the local Fleetwood-Hesketh family also to be found here.

Fire seems to have played an important role in the life of the town and one ancient custom still kept is Teanlay Night, which involves the lighting of bonfires on Hallowe'en. Each bonfire is encircled with white-coloured stones which are then thrown into the flames by the onlookers and left until the next day. The successful retrieval of one's own stone is considered a good omen for future prosperity.

Strolling around Poulton-le-Fylde now, it is hard to imagine that the town was once a seaport. But, until relatively recently ships sailed up the River Wyre to **Skippool Creek**. Today, the creek is home to the Blackpool and Fleetwood Yacht Club and from here the ocean-going yachts compete in major races around Britain.

The town had a rail link long before Blackpool and it was here that the early holidaymakers alighted from their trains to take a horse and trap the remaining few miles. Fortunately for Poulton, in 1846, the railway reached Blackpool and the town could, once again, return to a more peaceful existence. It is this quiet and charm, as well as sensitive approaches to planning, that have led it to become, in recent years, a much sought after residential area for businessmen now able to travel the M55 to Manchester and Liverpool.

Singleton   *Map 1 ref C7*
5 miles E of Blackpool on B5260

A quiet little Fylde village, **St Anne's Church**, built in 1860 by Thomas Miller, has, in its sanctuary, a black oak chair which bears the inscription 'John Milton, author of Paradise Lost and Paradise Regained 1671'. Opposite the building is the lych gate to the previous church which stood on this site.

Thomas Miller was a member of the Miller family who made their fortune, during the 19th century, in the cotton mills of Preston. Their home, Singleton Hall, lies tucked away out of sight behind a pair of impressive gates. The house is not open to the public.

Great Eccleston   *Map 1 ref C7*
8 miles E of Blackpool off A586

This quiet traditional agricultural community, on the banks of the River Wyre was, during the 17th and 18th centuries known locally as Little London as it was the social centre for the surrounding area. This was probably directly linked to the number of public houses and inns in the village at that time.

Every Wednesday, a bustling open air market is held in the charming village square. However, unlike most markets Great Eccleston's first took place in 1974 following a campaign started by the parish council a few years previously. The wide variety of stalls attract visitors from not only the immediate surroundings but also coaches from outside the rural area.

St Michael's on Wyre   *Map 1 ref D7*
10 miles E of Blackpool on A586

The River Wyre, at this point, is still tidal and, for centuries, the inhabitants of St Michael's and other villages in the area have suffered the threat of flooding. An old flood bank has been constructed from the village's bridge and below, beyond the overgrown banks, are the fertile fields of the flood plain.

Mentioned in the Domesday Book as Michelscherche, is it likely that the first church in the village was founded in the 7th century. As well as the many memorials to the Butler family, the church also contains a splendid 14th century mural that was only discovered in 1956 when repair work was being undertaken in the sanctuary.

The Butler family, whose home - Rawcliffe Hall - lies a few miles down river, have been known to have been in this area for 800 years and their house is built on the site of a Saxon dwelling. Another of the staunchly Catholic Lancashire families, the Butlers finally lost their house and the influence that they had in the area. The house is now part of a private country club.

Churchtown   *Map 1 ref D7*
12 miles E of Blackpool on A586

This delightful village has many buildings of both architectural and historic interest and none more so than the **Church of St Helen** which dates back to the days of the Norman Conquest. Featuring architectural styles from almost every period since the 11th century, this church is well worth exploring. The oldest parts of the building are the circular pillars near the nave which date from around 1200 and the roof is the original Tudor structure. Built on the site of a Saxon church, St Helen's is dedicated to the mother of Emperor Constantine and the circular churchyard is typical of the Saxon period.

Known as the **Cathedral of the Fylde**, the church has been subjected to flooding by the River Wyre and, in 1746, such was the damage caused by the rising waters that the rebuilding of the church looked necessary. However, the builder brought in to survey the scene, suggested that moving the river would be a cheaper option and this method of preserving the church was undertaken. The original course of the river can be seen by taking the footpath from the churchyard in the direction of the new river course.

Bilsborrow   *Map 1 ref D7*
12 miles E of Blackpool on A6

To the southeast of Churchtown, at Bilsborrow, can be found **The Roebuck Hotel**, an old established inn of many years standing, that will be known to many who have travelled the old main route to Lancaster from southern Lancashire along the A6. In the 19th century, the inn was also frequented by engine drivers and firemen who would slip in here for a toothful while waiting for the next train travelling the single track line.

Today, the Roebuck, managed by Kath and Brian Taylor, is still providing excellent food and drink all day, every day, to both local people and those passing through. Recently refurbished in a style

The Roebuck Hotel

sympathetic with the age of the building, the memorabilia displayed on the walls adds to the olde worlde atmosphere that has been created. As well as offering customers an excellent range of real ales and beers, The Roebuck Hotel also has a delicious menu of bar snacks and meals and once a month, for a week, there are themed menus. The exterior of the inn is decorated with colourful hanging baskets and window boxes in the summer months and The Roebuck lies adjacent to the village bowling green. *The Roebuck Hotel, Garstang Road, Bilsborrow, Lancashire PR3 0RN Tel: 01995 640234*

Woodplumpton   Map 1 ref D8
12 miles E of Blackpool off B5269

This charming little village, centred around its church, still has its well preserved village stocks, behind which is a mounting block that is now categorised as a historic monument. **St Anne's Church** is also a building of historic note and the keen-eyed will be quick to spot the octagonal cupola shape of tower that is reminiscent of the architecture of Christopher Wren. Completed in 1748, the tower was built to house a new timepiece, a clock, which replaced the sundial that for many years adorned the old tower. Bearing the date 1637, this can now be found in the churchyard.

Also in the churchyard is a huge boulder that is said to mark the grave of Margaret Hilton. Locally known as Meg Shelton she is best remembered as Meg the Witch! She lived in a cottage at nearby Catforth and, so it is said, she entered into a bet with her landlords, the Haydock family, that she could turn into a hare and outrun their dogs. This she did but one of the dogs managed to nearly catch up with the hare, biting its ankle as it fled back to Meg's cottage. From then on Meg not only limped but she was also, always, in a foul temper and was accused of turning milk sour and laming cattle. Apparently crushed between a water barrel and a well, her body was buried in the churchyard and to prevent it rising, the huge boulder was placed on top.

Barton   Map 1 ref D7
12 miles E of Blackpool off B5269

Barton Grange Hotel was originally built as a fine gentleman's residence in the early 1900s and was regarded as the epitome of elegance and refinement. The house was bought in 1945 by Edward and Ada Topping and opened as a hotel in 1950. Their grandson, Ian, now runs this quite exceptional establishment which was comprehensively refurbished in 1997. Following his motto, "Inspired by the Past. Created for the Future", Ian has sympathetically recap-

Barton Grange Hotel

tured the charm and character of the original house and successfully re-created the cosy Edwardian ambience of the Oak-panelled
Lounge by restoring many of the original features. At the same time,
guests are offered every modern amenity including a Leisure Centre with heated swimming pool, whirlpool, sauna and gym, a separate
games room, and a very well appointed hair and beauty salon.

A particularly attractive feature added during the 1997 refurbishment is The Garden Cafe-Bar Restaurant, ingeniously modelled
on plans for a walled garden, which Ian found amongst his grand-
mothers papers. Here, in delightful surroundings, visitors can enjoy
3-course meals with fine wine, light snacks, or some Lancastrian
specialities with a pint of ale. You won't be rushed because, as Ian
says, "We like people to linger awhile and enjoy the surroundings, -
that's what gardens are for!" *Barton Grange Hotel, Garstang Road,
Barton, near Preston, Lancashire PR3 5AA. Tel: 01772 862551*

Alongside Barton Grange Hotel, on the A6 at Barton, is the outstanding ***Barton Grange Garden Centre***. When, in 1963, Eddie
Topping set up his humble shop, 16 feet square, selling a limited
choice of plants with a modest selection of seeds and tools, little did
anyone think that it would, thirty years later, have grown into the
premier garden centre it is today.

Still owned and run by the Topping family, Barton Grange is the
place to come for anyone with an interest in plants. The staff, somewhat more numerous than in the early years, are experts in their
particular fields and always ready to help and offer advice. Everything you could possibly want for even the most modest garden can

Barton Grange Garden Centre

be found here, and it is a pleasure to wander around the various greenhouses and outdoor growing areas, marvelling at the wide variety of shrubs, trees and indoor plants on display. *Barton Grange Garden Centre, Garstang Road, Barton, near Preston, Lancashire, PR3 5AA Tel: 01772 864242*

Found down Station Lane, at Barton a couple of miles north of Woodplumpton, and situated on what was once the kitchen garden of the local manor house is **Newsham Nurseries**, home to one of the biggest alstroemeria nurseries in the north of England. It was not until 1986 that David Smith, a former toolmaker turned market gardener, first saw the lily-like alstroemeria, part Peruvian and part Inca lily, and began to cultivate them. Today, the flowers, which cannot breed, have taken over the nursery and David, with the help of his wife, Alice, and daughter, Susan, have a thriving family business on their hands. Popular with florists, particularly for wedding bouquets, these delicate flowers are often mistaken for orchids but they have a much longer vase life. Available in a wide variety of colours, these exotic plants have to be created from tissue culture,

Newsham Nurseries

where the cells are fused using a powerful electrical voltage. Open from dawn until dusk, David, a renowned expert on alstroemerias, is happy to welcome visitors wishing to see the queen of flowers. *Newsham Nurseries, Station Lane, Barton, Lancashire PR3 5DY Tel: 01772 864810*

Catforth
Map 1 ref D8

10 miles E of Blackpool off B5269

To the west of Woodplumpton, in the tucked away village of Catforth, can be found ***The Bay Horse*** which has been run by Beryl and Eric Hodgkinson since 1994. Prior to this the couple were stewards at the Kirkham Conservative Club so their credentials could not be better. Indeed, The Bay Horse is an excellent pub that is well worth finding. Originally built as a farmhouse, the premises became a pub in the 1930s and many of the features, including the three very

The Bay Horse

different fireplaces, give the establishment a cosy and comfortable feel, particularly when the fires are lit which is throughout the year - except during a heatwave! Open all day, every day, not only does The Bay Horse have an excellent selection of beers and ales behind the bar but a delicious range of tasty home-cooked bar snacks and meals are served at both lunchtime and in the evening (all day on Sundays). There is even a special children's menu to keep the whole family happy. In the summer, children, and adults too, will enjoy using the large beer garden at the rear of the premises and there are occasional quiz nights for those who like to test their general knowledge. *The Bay Horse, Catforth Road, Catforth, Lancashire PR4 0HH Tel: 01772 690389*

Clifton and Salwick   Map 1 ref D8
11 miles E of Blackpool off A583

Both Salwick and its neighbour, Clifton, were formed from part of the old Clifton estate. As well as the pleasant walks along the banks of the canal, visitors can also enjoy the delights of The Windmill pub which is, unlike most pubs of that name, housed in a converted windmill.

Hidden away in the village and beside the Lancaster Canal, is **The Hand and Dagger**, a charming country pub that is managed by Stephen, Natalie, Richard, and Pamela. Dating back to the late 17th century, this handsome pub was formerly called the Clifton Arms and, as well as changing its name, it is also the original Pig and Chicken Food House, so called as these are Stephen and Richard's nicknames. Open all day during in the summer, not only does The Hand and Dagger serve an excellent range of beers and ales but, as the two men are both chefs, there is a wonderful menu, featuring - as one might imagine - pork and chicken. As well as these

The Hand and Dagger

imaginatively prepared dishes, the extensive menu includes a variety of vegetarian options, salads, and other meats and fish as well as a selection of children's favourites. Certainly a very popular aspect of the pub, The Hand and Dagger also offers visitors the opportunity to sit outside in a lovely patio-style beer garden, there is a safe children's play area and, on Wednesday evenings, all are welcome to take part in the regular quiz night. *The Hand and Dagger, Pig and Chicken Food House, Treales Road, Salwick, Lancashire PR4 0SA Tel & Fax: 01772 690306*

Treales
Map 1 ref D8
9 miles E of Blackpool off A583

Although the M55 runs close by the village lies in an area of quiet country lanes, small woods, and farms. As well as the tastefully restored cottages, some of which have managed to retain their thatched roofs, this rural village's old windmill also has been converted into a beautiful home.

Kirkham
Map 1 ref C8
8 miles E of Blackpool off A583

Mentioned in the Domesday Book, there was a settlement here in Saxon times, known as Ciric-ham, and, before that, the Romans

Kirkham

had a fort though it is now lost under a modern housing estate. Kirkham was first granted a charter to hold a weekly market in 1296 and, since then, it has been serving the needs of the surrounding farming communities. The Fishstones are still to be seen; the flat stone slabs are set on stone uprights to form a semi-circle and were the counters from which fish was sold.

However, Kirkham was also touched by the Industrial Revolution and by the middle of the 18th century there were flax-spinning

mills and sailcloth was manufactured. By the 19th century, there were also come cotton mills.

Wrea Green
Map 1 ref C8
6 miles E of Blackpool on B5259

A picturesque old village, Wrea Green has not only retained its village green, complete with duck pond, but it is still the focus for the community.

Freckleton
Map 1 ref C9
9 miles E of Blackpool on A584
This old Fylde village's name is derived from the Anglo-Saxon Frecheltun meaning 'an enclosed area' and this is how it featured in the Domesday Book. Situated on the northern banks of the River Ribble, the long straggling village was, until the river was canalised, surrounded by marshland. It is here, perhaps more so than anywhere that the name Fylde seems so appropriate as it comes from the Anglo-Saxon word 'gefilde' which means level green fields.

Lytham St Anne's
Map 1 ref B9
4 miles E of Blackpool on A584
Situated on the coast, Lytham St Anne's is, in fact, two towns which now share their name but have quite distinctive characteristics. Linked together in 1923, St Anne's evolved in just over a century whilst Lytham was mentioned in the Domesday Book. Before the development of the resort, in the Victorian age, Lytham was an important port on the Ribble estuary and it was home to the first fishing company on this stretch of the northwest coast. Shipbuilding also continued here until the 1950s, when the last vessel constructed in the shipyards was the Windermere Car Ferry. During the 1940s, parts of the famous Mulberry harbour were constructed in secret in preparation for the invasion of Normandy in 1944.

The arrival of the railway, linking Lytham with Preston, prompted a group of Lancashire businessmen to plan the construction of a health resort between the old established port and the rapidly expanding town of Blackpool to the north. There was scarcely a cottage on their chosen site when, in 1875, the work began but the growth of the carefully planned town was spectacular. In just 30 years the population increased from 1,000 to 17,000 inhabitants.

The **Promenade**, running the full length of the seafront from St Anne's to Lytham was constructed in 1875 and, on the landward side, there are several fine examples of Victorian and Edwardian seaside villas. Beyond the attractive Promenade Gardens, laid out by a local character, Henry Gregson, is **St Anne's Pier**. Opened in 1885, the elegant pier was built in a mock Tudor style and, up until 1897, fishing smacks and pleasure boats were able to tie up at the end of the jetty. Lytham also had a pier, built in 1865, but during a gale in 1903, two sand barges dragged their anchors and sliced the structure in two. Undeterred, and with the Pavilion still standing at the far end the pier was rebuilt only to be almost entirely destroyed by fire in 1928.

In fact, the town has had its fair share of disasters associated with the sea but, by far the worst, occurred in 1886 and it is still Britain's greatest lifeboat disaster. The crew of the St Anne's lifeboat, with the help of the Southport lifeboat, set out to answer a distress signal put up by a German ship, the Mexico. During the rescue some 15 lifeboat crew were lost and the tragedy led to the improvement of lifeboat design. Situated in the *Alpine Garden*, on the Promenade, is a monument which pays tribute to the men who lost their lives. The statue features the stone figure of a coxswain looking out to sea with a rope in one hand and a lifebelt in the other.

As well as being an elegant place full of fine Victorian and Edwardian architecture, Lytham St Anne's also contains some reminders to the more distant past. *Lytham Hall*, now privately owned by a large insurance company, started life as a farming cell of the Durham cathedral in 1190. After the Reformation, the estate changed hands several times, until, in 1606, it became the property of Sir Cuthbert Clifton, the first squire of Lytham. The fine Georgian hall standing today was the building that John Carr of York built for Thomas Clifton between 1757 and 1764. The extensive grounds, once part of the estate, is now *Lytham Hall Country Park*, where visitors can follow several nature trails to discover the birds and wildlife living here which includes three species of woodpecker, the lesser whitethroat, and the hawfinch.

There has been a *Windmill* at Lytham for over 800 years though the present structure dates from 1805. A well known landmark along the coast, the building has a solid white tower with a cap that looks rather like an upturned boat. In 1929, the wind set the four sails turning the wrong way, ruining the machinery and firing the mill, which has never worked since. Now renovated the windmill is home to a permanent exhibition on the building's history and on the process of breadmaking. Adjacent to the windmill, and the original home of the Lytham lifeboat, Old Lifeboat House is home to the *Lifeboat Museum*. Both buildings have limited opening times. Two other museums worthy of a visit are the *Lytham Motive Power Museum*, with its large model railway layout and an outdoor display of rolling stock, and the *Toy and Teddy Museum*, housed in the Porrit Victorian building with a varied collection of childhood memorabilia.

For those interested in discovering more about the abundant wildlife of the dune system here a visit to *Lytham St Anne's Nature Reserve* is a must. Established in 1968, the reserve is an important scientific site as well as being just a small part of what

Windmill, Lytham St Anne's

was once a very extensive sand dune system. As well as the rich plant life, the dunes are home to several rare species of migrating birds including osprey, black redstart, and Lapland buntings.

No description of Lytham St Anne's is complete without a mention of the **Royal Lytham and St Anne's Golf Course**. The club originated after a meeting, held in 1886, where a group of 19 keen golfers sought to furnish themselves with suitable facilities. The course opened in 1898 and it is still considered by many to be one of the finest golf links in the country and it is a regular host of the British Open.

CHAPTER FOUR
The Forests of Pendle and Rossendale

Newchurch

Chapter 4 - Area Covered

For precise location of places please refer to the colour maps found at the rear of the book.

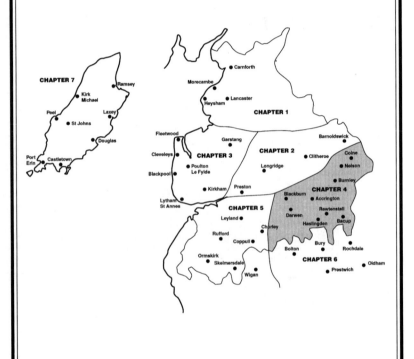

4
The Forests of Pendle and Rossendale

Introduction

Although during medieval times both the Forest of Pendle and the Forest of Rossendale were royal hunting grounds, these both relatively treeless areas have, since hunting ceased, developed along very different lines. Pendle, with the famous hill at its centre, is still an isolated stretch of moorland with few roads traversing the scene. Surrounding the higher ground are a series of untouched villages which, though they saw some industrialisation with the expansion of the textile industry, have still remained small.

To the southwest of Pendle Hill lies Whalley, a picturesque village, save for the giant railway viaduct, that is home to one of the best preserved abbeys in the country. The southern edge of the Pendle area is centred around the valley of Colne Water and here are the famous textile towns of Burnley, Nelson, and Colne.

Further south, the larger area, the Forest of Rossendale saw the establishment of no real settlements until the 1400s, when the Crown leased off parts of the forest, and the early 1500s, when the final clearance and deforestation began.

During the course of the 18th century, important advances in textile technology brought the introduction of water-powered mills to Rossendale. At this time cotton was also being imported and took over from the traditional woollen cloth manufacture. During the second half of the 19th century the industrial prosperity was so great that Rossendale came known as the Golden Valley.

With Blackburn, one of the area's oldest settlements, in the north and Rawtenstall, Darwen, and Bacup in the centre of what was the forest, the whole region was a hive of activity, both making and finishing the cloth with others providing the necessary support. However, Rossendale, though provided with a much better road system, still offers tremendous opportunities for outdoor leisure and recreation as well, of course, as a fascinating industrial history.

Burnley

This cotton town is rich in history as well as being the largest town in this area of East Lancashire. Incorporating some 50 square miles, the town offers visitors a wealth of contrasts, from some of the best preserved industrial landscapes in Britain to the magnificent, untouched moorlands just to the east. First established at the beginning of the 9th century, the town nestles in a basin between the River Calder and the River Brun, from which it takes its name.

With the Industrial Revolution and the building of the Leeds and Liverpool Canal, Burnley not only expanded but grew in stature until, by the end of the 19th century, it was the world's leading producer of cotton cloth. A walk along the towpath of the canal, through an area known as the *Weavers' Triangle* is like taking a step back in time. This is an area of spinning mills and weaving sheds; foundries where steam engines and looms were made; canal-side warehouses; domestic buildings, including a unique row of workers' cottages; and a Victorian school house. The Weavers' Triangle Visitors Centre is housed in the former wharfemaster's house and canal toll office. The centre is open to the public on several afternoons a week during the summer months and on most bank holidays.

The history of Burnley can also be explored by boat along the Leeds and Liverpool Canal. This famous waterway leaves the Weavers' Triangle via a huge embankment which carries the canal across the town. Known as the 'straight mile', it is in fact less than that but no less exciting and, at 60 feet above the ground, it is one of the most impressive features of the canal's length.

Situated on the Todmorden Road on the outskirts of Burnley, the *Towneley Hall Art Gallery and Museum*. The home of the Towneley family since the 14th century, right up until 1902, parts of the present building date from the 15th century. Visitors can not only view the art collections, the Whalley Abbey Vestments, and the museum of local crafts and industries, but also take in a tour of the house. The kitchens, with their open fires, the servants' hall, and the fascinating family rooms are all on display. The grounds too are open to visitors and there are facilities for golf, tennis, bowls, and other outdoor pursuits.

Two other interesting places to visit whilst in Burnley are the **Burnley Heritage Centre**, where memorabilia on display from the town's past includes old photographs, a Lancashire loom, and a replica 1930s kitchen and living room. **The Stables Museum**, open at the weekends, is one of the town's newest attractions and can be found at the wharf. Run by the Horses and Ponies Protection Association, the museum is a must for horse lovers and the exhibitions include information of the rescue and care of neglected horses, ponies, and donkeys as well as a display of the life of the canal horse.

North of Burnley

Brierfield   Map 3 ref H7
2 miles N of Burnley on A682

This industrial town has magnificent views of Pendle Hill as it lies on a steep slope at the bottom of which is an attractive **Quaker Bridge** over Pendle Water. At the beginning of the 19th century, coal was discovered in the area and, within a few years, three pits had opened, thus sealing Brierfield's fate as a place of industry. The laying of turnpike roads, followed by the opening of the Leeds and Liverpool Canal, gave the growing village a further boost and, by 1833, a handloom weaving business was also flourishing here. The humid climate and expanding transport system made Brierfield an ideal place for the bludgeoning cotton industry, which had become the main source of employment here by the end of the 19th century.

Nelson   Map 3 ref I7
3 miles N of Burnley on A56

This town, along with its neighbour, Colne, and Burnley are now inseparable as they share the same valley running along the length of Colne Water. Nelson is a modern textile town which takes its name from the hotel, The Lord Nelson, which stands by the railway line running along the valley bottom. However, although the town itself might have been the product of the Industrial Age, two of its suburbs, Little and Great Marsden, have been here for centuries. Here, above Nelson, lies **Marsden Park**, and once Marsden Hall, the home of the de Walton family until their line died out in 1912. Acquired by the local authority, much of the hall was demolished whilst the parkland was developed.

Colne

Map 3 ref I7

5 miles N of Burnley on A56

Before the Industrial Revolution turned this area into a valley devoted to the production of cotton cloth, Colne was a small market town that specialised in wool. Unfortunately, there are few reminders to the days before industrialisation but **St Batholomew's Church**, founded in 1122, is still here and contains some interesting interior decorations and furnishings. In the centre of the town, next to the War Memorial is another memorial. The statue is of Lawrence Hartley, the bandmaster on the ill-fated *Titanic* who, heroically, stayed at his post with his musicians and played 'Nearer my God to Thee' as the liner sank beneath the waves of the icy Atlantic in 1912.

Colne is also the unlikely home of the **British in India Museum**, where exhibits covering many aspects of the British rule over the subcontinent, from the 17th century until 1947, can be seen.

Wycoller

Map 3 ref I7

6 miles NE of Burnley off B6250

This hamlet lies amidst the moorlands that rise to the east of the textile towns of the Colne valley and up to the bleak summits of the Pennines. Now almost deserted, this was once a thriving place as an important centre for the wool trade and as a handloom weavers' settlement but it lost most of its inhabitants to the new factories in the west.

Fortunately, the place has been saved by the creation of a **Wycoller Country Park**, surrounding the village, and many of the buildings have been restored. There is also a delightful old humpbacked packhorse bridge crossing a stream and, above the village, a single slab gritstone bridge, **Clam Bridge**, that is thought to date from the Iron Age. Now a ruin, **Wycoller Hall** was the inspiration for Ferndean Manor in Charlotte Brontë's *Jane Eyre*: Wycoller was one of the villages to which the sisters walked from their house at Haworth.

Foulridge

Map 3 ref I7

6 miles NE of Burnley off A56

Originally a Quaker Meeting House, **The New Inn** has an elevated position down a quiet side street in Foulridge.Dating back to the 17th century, this interesting building has witnessed many things and it even has its own ghost.Known locally as Tommy, he is believed to be a Quaker ghost and to have come from the Quaker Burial

The New Inn

Ground close by. The building was converted into a pub in 1889 and the plans for the work can be seen hanging on the wall inside.They make interesting reading as does another document telling the history of the pub which also goes on to explain how the village got its name.

This traditional pub is managed by landlord and lady, Barry and Barbara who have created a wonderful, relaxed and friendly pub which not only provides a popular meeting place for the locals but also welcomes visitors. Lying close to the Leeds and Liverpool Canal and within easy reach of many local attractions, the New Inn is also popular with walkers, cyclists, tourists, and those cruising the canal. Famous for their Steak and Hard, a traditional Lancashire dish, Barry and Barbara served excellent, freshly prepared, home-cooked food along with a good selection of beers.The pub's occasional Pie and Peas evenings are also well worth looking out for and should not be missed. *The New Inn, Skipton Old Road, Foulridge, near Colne, Lancashire BB8 7PD Tel: 01282 864068*

Earby   Map 3 ref I6
10 miles NE of Burnley on A56
The town lies almost on the county border with Yorkshire and here can be found the **Earby Mines Museum** housed in the old Grammar School building. With the largest collection of lead mining tools and equipment used in the Yorkshire Dales on display, there is much to see, including examples of the minerals extracted, a lead crushing mill, and other working models.

Pendle Hill   *Map 3 ref H7*
5 miles N of Burnley off A6068

A constant feature of the skyline in this part of Lancashire, this great whaleback mountain lends into name to the ancient hunting ground and region it still dominates. The hill, and the surrounding tiny villages, have a rich history and, due to the isolation, there are

View from Pendle Hill

also many legends: none more well known than the tragic story of the Pendle Witches. The infamous witches were, in the main, old women who dabbled with plants and herbs, knowing which could heal and which, when ingested, would spell certain death.

The early 17th century was a time of superstition and fear and, in 1612, several of the women were imprisoned in Lancaster Castle as a result of their seemingly evil practices. At the trial, chilling accounts of witchcraft came to light as families and neighbours accused each other of wrongdoing. Later that year, on August 10th, 10 women and one of their sons were found guilty of witchcraft and were hanged in front of huge crowds. Though, as a rule, witches tended to come from the poorer elements of society, one of the women, Alice Nutter, was said to be rich with a sizeable estate. A few years later, in 1633, there were further trials and, whilst some of the accused died in prison, four prisoners were taken to London and put on show.

To the west of the hill's summit lies **Apronfull Hill**, a Bronze Age burial site, that is said to be the place from which the Devil threw stones at Clitheroe Castle, creating what is known as the Devil's window.

Something of this old, dark tragedy still broods over Pendle and many memories and places which hark back to those grim days remain. Those interested in finding out more about the trials should visit the **Pendle Heritage Centre** at **Barrowford**, to the southeast of the hill. Historically, witches aside, the hill was one of the many beacon hills throughout the country that, forming a chain, were lit in times of national crisis, such as the sighting of the Spanish Armada.

Newchurch
Map 3 ref H7
4 miles N of Burnley off A6068

This charming Pendle village was named after John Bird, Bishop of Chester, who consecrated a new church here in 1544. Earlier, during the Middle Ages, Newchurch was a cow and deer rearing centre, as well as part of the old hunting forest of Pendle but, by the reign of Elizabeth I, the area was becoming deforested and farming was beginning to take over as the primary source of income.

Newchurch did not escape from stories of witchcraft that surrounded the notorious Pendle witches trial in the 17th century, and many ghostly tales and shadowy traditions are said to be associated

Newchurch

with the village. Though those times were a frightening experience for anyone living in the area, by the 18th century, the witch hunts were over and the village grew rapidly as part of the expanding textile industry, first with handloom weavers and then with the construction of a factory for washing and dyeing wool.

Found on the main street in this pretty village is *The Boar's Head*, an imposing public house that dates from 1674. As well as having been an inn for a considerable length of time, the upper storey of the building was, many years ago, used as a magistrates' court.

The Boar's Head

Today, this charming village pub is managed by Maureen and Tony O'Connor, who also live above, and Maureen has worked behind the bar here for many years. Well decorated and furnished and with a real homely atmosphere, not only can customers expect to find a range of excellent real ales here but also a delicious menu of meals and bar snacks, which are served at both lunchtime and in the evening. With a quiz night every Thursday evening and occasional live music to which all are welcome, this is very much a centre of village life. To the rear of the premises, there is also an attractive beer garden, a must in the summer, and a bowling green. *The Boar's Head, 69 Church Street, Newchurch, Lancashire BB4 9EH Tel: 01706 214687*

West of Burnley

Padiham   *Map 3 ref H8*
2 miles W of Burnley on A646
This charming small town of narrow winding lanes and cobbled alleyways, still retains characteristics typical of the early days of the

Industrial Revolution. However, there was a settlement here long before the Norman Conquest and Padiham was also the market town for the western slopes of Pendle.

Padiham is also the home of ***Gawthorpe Hall***, which lies to the east of the town. A splendid 17th century house, it was restored with a flourish of Victorian elegance during the 1850s by Sir Charles Barry. Although Gawthorpe Hall had been the home of the

Gawthorpe Hall

Shuttleworth family since the early 15th century, work on the construction of the present hall only started in 1600. Open to the public, the beautiful period furnishings are enhanced by the ornately decorated ceilings and the original wood panelled walls, which also provide the perfect setting for the nationally important Kay-Shuttleworth needlework and lace collection.

Read   *Map 3 ref G8*

5 miles W of Burnley on A671

Situated on the banks of the River Calder it was during a skirmish near ***Read Old Bridge***, in April 1643, that the Royalist cause in Lancashire was lost.

Read Hall, privately owned and no longer in the hands of the original family, was the home of one of Lancashire's most famous

families, the Nowells. It was Roger Nowell, in 1612, who committed the Pendle witches to trial. The Nowells left the hall in 1772
and, in 1799, the house was completely rebuilt in the Georgian style
seen today.

Whalley
Map 3 ref G7

7 miles W of Burnley on B6246

This is a charming village, full of character, that has changed little
over the centuries. Although it is now somewhat dominated by the
49-arch railway viaduct, Whalley has a much older history which
dates back to the 13th century and the time when **Whalley Abbey**
was founded by Cistercian monks. In fact, Whalley was not the
monks' first choice as they had already set up a religious house at
Stanlow, on the banks of the River Mersey and now under a huge oil
refinery, in 1172.

Seeking somewhere
with less harsh and more
fertile land, the monks
moved to Whalley in 1296
but their attempts to build
were hampered as Sawley
Abbey felt threatened by
the competition for the do-
nations of land and goods
expected from the local
population. Building fi-
nally began in 1310 and, by
1400, the imposing and impressive abbey had taken
shape. The demise of the
abbey came, as it did to all
religious houses, under
Henry VIII but Whalley's
abbot, joining forces with
the abbot of Sawley, took
part in the Pilgrimage of
Grace in an attempt to
save their houses. This
failed and the abbots were
both executed.

Whalley Abbey

Now owned and cared for by the Diocese of Blackburn, Whalley
Abbey is one of the best preserved such places in the country and its
future secure as it also acts as a conference centre.

Whalley's **Parish Church**, dating from the 13th century, is also well worth a visit. Built on the site of an older place of worship, the churchyard is home to three ancient crosses and the church itself contains a set of the some of the finest choir stalls anywhere. They were brought here from the abbey after the Dissolution and though they are not elaborate there are some intriguing carvings on the lower portions.

The Dog Inn on the main street dates back, in parts, to the 17th century but there first appeared a licensed premises of that name in the Town Census in 1830. Formerly a farmhouse, the farm outbuildings can still be seen at the rear of the pub and, even now, the stables are home to several horses.

Personally run for the past six years by Norman and Christine Atty, the couple are always on hand to ensure that all visitors receive a warm welcome at the Dog Inn. Pretty as a picture inside, the low ceilings and open fires all add to the olde worlde atmosphere. Memorabilia decorates the walls and, amongst the many items on

The Dog Inn

show, the keen eyed will spot sporting scenes and old coaching posters. At lunchtime food is available with the menu displayed on three blackboards. Cooked to order and absolutely delicious, customers can enjoy their home-cooked meal whilst listening to the classical music playing in the background. Diners should note that the Dog Inn also has a fine reputation for its home-made soups and puddings. In the evenings, Norman and Christine happily welcome those new to the area who drop in to the pub for an informal drink and a chat with the locals. There is a good selection of beers from which to choose as well as a fine selection of wines on offer. Food can also be served in the evenings if it has been ordered in advance by telephone. *The Dog Inn, King Street, Whalley, Lancashire BB7 9SP Tel: 01254 823009*

With many places of interest to visit around Whalley what better place to aim for refreshments than **The Toby Jug Tea Shop** on King Street. This is a quaint Grade H listed building with oak beams and panelling from the abbey which authenticates its age and adds a special touch to the homely atmosphere of the tea shop. Opened in 1985, the business soon developed and it has earned a good reputation for its home-made fruit pies, cakes, and traditional afternoon

The Toby Jug Tea Shop

teas. Although the selection changes regularly, the walnut cake, lemon gateau, and fresh cream cakes remain firm favourites. Wholemeal sandwiches of home-cooked chicken and ham with salad are freshly made to order and the extensive menu offers further selections of home-made soups and speciality lunches. Although the owners are delighted to welcome visitors any time, the weekdays offer a more relaxed pace. There is good wheelchair access and The Toby Jug Tea Shop is also a no-smoking premises. Closed on Sundays and Mondays. *The Toby Jug Tea Shop, 20 King Street, Whalley, Lancashire Tel: 01254 823298*

Pendleton
Map 3 ref G7

6 miles NW of Burnley off A59

Recorded in the Domesday Book when the village was part of the vast parish of Whalley, this small settlement of cottages and working farms has retained much of its traditional air. However, the discovery of a Bronze Age burial urn in the village would indicate that there were settlers here as long ago as 1600 BC.

From the village there is a steep road, to the southeast, that climbs up to the **Nick of Pendle** from where there are magnificent views.

Rishton
Map 3 ref G8

7 miles W of Burnley on A678

Originally a Saxon settlement, the name means the fortified village or dwelling place amid the rushes, and, during the Middle Ages, the village grew in importance as an early textile centre with the operation of its fulling mill. By the 17th century, Rishton had gained a name for the manufacture of linen cloth and, in 1766, it became the first village to weave calico. As the Industrial Revolution advanced, the industry moved from the weavers' homes into newly built mills.

The manor of Rishton, once owned by the Petre family, was part of the larger estate of Clayton-le-Moors and the manor house, **Dunkenhalgh Hall**, is said to have been named after a Scottish raider called Duncan who made his home here. Elizabethan in origin, the hall is now a private hotel.

Oswaldtwistle
Map 3 ref G9

7 miles W of Burnley on A679

This typical Lancashire textile town could be considered to be at the heart of the industry since it was whilst staying here, at what is now Stanhill Post Office, that James Hargreaves invented his famous 'Spinning Jenny' in 1764. Although he was forced to leave the area after, sometimes violent, opposition to his machine from local hand spinners, the town's prosperity is largely due to textiles and, in particular, calico printing. However, Oswaldtwistle is a much older settlement than its rows of Victorian terraced houses would suggest as the name means the boundary of the kingdom of Oswald, who was a 7th century Northumbrian king.

Great Harwood
Map 3 ref G8

6 miles W of Burnley on B6535

Before the Industrial Revolution, this was a quiet village of farms and cottages nestling between two streams. Famous for its fine woollen cloth, at the beginning of the 19th century cotton handloom weaving and then, by the 1850s, the introduction of the factory system and the cotton mills took over. Although only one mill remains, at the industry's height, the town supported 22 mills. Not surprisingly, Great Harwood's most famous son was very much linked with cotton. In 1850, John Mercer, an industrial chemist, developed the technique of processing cotton to give it a sheen and the technique, mercerisation, is still used today. The free-standing clock tower found in the Town Square was erected in 1903 to commemorate Mercer's contribution to the life of his home town.

Situated in the heart of Great Harwood, the 17th century *Walmesley Arms* is a charming, atmospheric pub that has been serving the drinking needs of the town for many years. Today's landlord, Simon O'Rouke, carries on the tradition by ensuring that

The Walmesley Arms

there is always a fine selection of real ales as well as other beers, lagers, ciders, and stouts on hand. Very much a locals' pub, this is certainly the place to come to for the latest local news and gossip as well as a quiet chat after a hard day's work. New faces are also made welcome and entertainment, in the form of the ever popular Kareoke, is a feature on Thursday evenings and Sunday late afternoons. *The Walmesley Arms, 26 Queen Street, Great Harwood, Lancashire BB6 7QQ Tel: 01254 886889*

The Lidgett Hotel, found on the outskirts of the town, dates back to the late 19th century and is unusual in having a stream running beneath the building. However, this and the pub's previous name, The Cemetery, has not hindered the landlords, Mary and Roy Hindle, in turning The Lidgett into one of the area's most popular establish-

The Lidgett Hotel

ments. As attractive inside as it is from the outside, the pub not only has a fine selection of excellent beers and ales, as well as ciders, lagers, and stouts, but also a tasty range of bar snacks and meals are served right up to closing time. Well frequented by locals, visitors are made very welcome and, to add to customers enjoyment and entertainment, there is live music on the occasional Saturday evening. *The Lidgett Hotel, 244 Blackburn Road, Great Harwood, Lancashire BB6 7LX Tel: 01254 882642*

Accrington   *Map 3 ref G9*
5 miles SW of Burnley on A680
This attractive Victorian market town, as is typical in this area, expanded as a result of the increase in the textile industry of the 18th and 19th centuries. The town is the home of the **Haworth Art Gallery**, one of the most attractive in the country as it is set in beautiful parkland, which houses the largest collection of Tiffany

glass - there are 130 pieces - in Europe. The collection was presented to the town by Joseph Briggs, an Accrington man, who went to New York to work with Louis Tiffany for nearly 40 years. Briggs joined the studio in 1890 and rose through the company ranks to become the manager of the Mosaic department before, finally, becoming Tiffany's personal assistant.

After the First World War, the fashion for Tiffany glassware waned and, during the economic depression of the 1920s, Briggs was given the sad job of selling off the remainder of the Tiffany stock. Returning to his native Accrington in 1933 with his collection of glass, Briggs gave half to the town and distributed the remainder amongst his family.

South of Burnley

Bacup *Map 3 ref I9*

7 miles S of Burnley on A671

Built in the 19th century for the sole purpose of cotton manufacture, Bacup remains one of the best examples of a textile town in England even though it suffered more than most when the mills began to close. Any stroll through the town centre will reveal carefully restored shops and houses, with the grander homes of the mill owners and the elegant civic buildings acting as a reminder of the town's more prosperous times.

An excellent time to visit the town is during the Easter weekend when the town's famous troop of Morris dancers take to the streets. Known as the **Coconut Dancers**, their costume is unique and involves wearing halved coconut husks strapped to their knees and blackening their faces. Maintaining that the correct name is Moorish, not Morris, Dancers, the tradition is thought to go back to the times of the Crusades.

Found in the heart of this old Lancashire town, **O'Dwyer's Bar**, which was formerly known as the Market Hotel, dates back to the mid-1870s. A friendly pub, that has been catering to the needs of both locals and visitors for many years, this is an excellent town pub that has maintained its traditional Victorian inn feel. Not only does much of the building's original panel work remain in place but the addition of old prints and displays of memorabilia add to the olde worlde atmosphere. The hospitality, led by landlord David Parker, is equally good and as well as ensuring that there is an excellent range of well-kept ales at the bar, David is happy to cater

to the needs of any visitors who are hungry - rustling up anything from a sandwich to a steak. The Sunday lunchtime roasts are also very popular. This is a lively place with some form of entertainment on each evening, from Kareoke and live music to darts and pool. The hospitality does not, however, end with the food, drink, and entertainment as O'Dwyer's Bar also has five comfortable bedrooms and children too are welcome. O'Dwyer's Bar, 14 Market Street, Bacup,

O'Dwyer's Bar

Lancashire OL13 8ZN Tel: 01706 873116

Found a couple of miles north of Bacup, on the road to Burnley and surrounded by glorious countryside, **The Deerplay Inn** is a lovely family-run pub. The inn's unusual name comes from the deer that once lived in the Forest of Rossendale and were seen on nearby Deerplay Hill. Dating back to the 18th century, this former coaching inn is run by a well-known local man, Jim Cropper. The winner

The Deerplay Inn

of many sheep dog trials, including the International Double Dogs Competition in 1972 and One Man and His Dog (Doubles) in 1987, Jim also judges around the world and photographs of his successes can be seen in the pub.

The inn is open every day, all day at the weekends, and, as well as the excellent range of ales, there is also a fine menu of tasty bar snacks and meals which is supplemented by a daily specials' board. Outside is a safe play area for the children and, also in the grounds of the pub, not only is there the start of the River Irwell but also sheep, cows, and pigs are reared free range. A lively pub, with a well established reputation for the superb hospitality offered to all visitors, this is certainly a place well worth finding. *The Deerplay Inn, Burnley Road, Bacup, Lancashire OL13 8RD Tel: 01706 873109*

Rawtenstall
Map 3 ref H9
7 miles S of Burnley on A682
The town first developed as a centre of the woollen cloth trade with the work being undertaken by hand workers in their own homes before steam-powered mills were introduced in the early 19th century. The introduction of the cotton industry to the town happened at around the same time. Lower Mill, now a ruin, was opened in 1840 by the Whitehead brothers who were some of the area's first manufacturing pioneers. The **Weaver's Cottage**, purpose built for a home weaver, is one of the last buildings remaining of its kind and it is open to visitors at weekends during the summer.

Also in the town, and housed in a former Victorian mill owner's house called Oakhill, is the **Rossendale Museum**. Naturally, the area's industrial heritage is given a prominent position but collections of the region's natural history, fine art and furniture, and ceramics are on display too.

At one end of the town stands a new railway station which marks the end of a very old railway line - the **East Lancashire Railway**. Opened in 1846 and run commercially until 1980, when the last coal train drew into Rawtenstall, the line is now in the hands of the East Lancashire Railway Preservation Society. Running a passenger service (at weekends with additional summer services), the steam trains offer an enthralling 17 mile round trip along the River Irwell between Rawtenstall and Bury, via Ramsbottom.

Helmshore
Map 3 ref H10
8 miles S of Burnley on B6214
This small town still retains much evidence of the early Lancashire cotton industry and, housed in an old cotton mill, is the Museum of

the Lancashire Textile Industry, **Higher Mill Museum**. The building dates from 1789 and it was one of the first fulling mills to be built in the Rossendale area.

Haslingden
Map 3 ref H9
7 miles S of Burnley on A56

The market in this town, which serves much of the Rossendale Valley, dates back to 1676, when the charter was granted by Charles II. Tuesdays and Fridays, market days, still bring the town alive as people flock to the numerous stalls.

With such an interest in antiques and curios these days, a stop at **Something Old Something New** is a must for anyone looking for a gift with a difference or an addition to their home. The shop, owned and personally managed by Donna and Peter Kelly, is housed

Something Old Something New

in an early 19th century building and inside there is an extensive array of period furniture, antiques, attractive pottery, pictures, and interesting curios. The couple also have an excellent selection of Hannah and Alberon limited edition porcelain dolls. Gift opportunities are everywhere and browsers will enjoy the challenge of seeking out that special find. Something Old Something New is open every day except Wednesday when Donna and Peter can be found at their stall in Burnley market. *Something Old Something New, 30 Blackburn Road, Haslingden, Lancashire BB4 5QQ Tel: 01706 221976*

The Regent Hotel, tucked away behind Haslingden's main road, is a late 17th century former coaching house whose rear stables were, for many years, home to the Rossendale Pigeon Fanciers Club and it was here that the pigeons were docked after racing. Though the pigeons have gone, this excellent pub, managed since February 1998 by Barbara and Albert, is still offering hospitality to locals and visitors alike. Essentially a wet pub, with a good selection of ales behind the bar, the couple are happy to rustle up sandwiches for hungry customers. However, beer is not the only thing on offer at The Regent Hotel as Barbara and Albert have a full list of afternoon and evening entertainments throughout the week, including live music on Friday nights and Sunday afternoons, Kareoke on Monday afternoons and Saturday evenings, and a quiz on

The Regent Hotel

Wednesday evening. Children too will enjoy the small aviary that Barbara and Albert have built in the courtyard. *The Regent Hotel, 10 Regent Street, Haslingden, Lancashire BB4 5HQ Tel: 01706 214000*

Crawshawbooth
Map 3 ref H9

5 miles SW of Burnley on A682

Once an important settlement in the old hunting forest of Rossendale, the village's oldest house, **Swinshaw Hall** (now privately owned), is said to have played a part in the destruction of the last wild boar in England. The influence of non-conformists can also still be seen in the village, where a number made their home, in the old **Quaker Meeting House** dating from 1716.

With lovely views overlooking the Rossendale Valley, **The Jester** is a popular well-known local pub that is managed by Yvonne and John. Some time ago, the couple used to manage the pub but they moved away; local customers so missed Yvonne and John that they requested the brewery ask the couple to return, which they did in 1994. Since then nobody has looked back and The Jester has gone from strength to strength. As well as the fine range of ales, including an old Burnley brew Massey's Bitter, this is the place to come

The Jester

for excellent, home-cooked food which is served all day. The atmosphere inside this early 19th century pub is warm and friendly and there is plenty going on with a quiz on Wednesday evenings and live music on Saturday nights. To the rear of the premises is a large beer garden, with glorious panoramic views of Lancashire's hill country, and also crazy golf. A great place for the whole family where everyone is sure to feel at home. *The Jester, 810 Burnley Road, Crawshawbooth, Lancashire BB4 8BH Tel: 01706 215809*

Goodshaw   *Map 3 ref H9*
5 miles S of Burnley on A682

Just to the north of Crawshawbooth in the small village of Goodshaw and set high above the main road lies Goodshaw Chapel, a recently restored Baptist house of worship that dates from 1760.

Standing opposite the Parish Church of St Mary and All Saints, as might be imagined, **The Old White Horse** was, until the early

The Old White Horse

1960s, a public house. However, today, this charming 200 year-old building is the home of Maggie and John Clegg who, in the 20 or so years that they have been here, have completely renovated and refurbished the building to the high standard it is now. The original bar is all that remains of The Old White Horse's past life but this is still the place to come for excellent hospitality as Maggie and John offer superb bed and breakfast accommodation in three comfortable rooms. Very much a family home, guests will find everything they could possible need has been thoughtfully provided and there are delightful additional touches like the splendid quilts and cushions that have been hand-made and quilted by Maggie.

With its elevated position, looking towards the Rossendale Valley, The Old White Horse is popular with walkers and there is a marvellous home-cooked breakfast to set everyone up for a day exploring. Packed lunches can be provided and delicious evening meals are available on request. *The Old White Horse, 211 Goodshaw Lane, Goodshaw, Lancashire BB4 8DD Tel: 01706 215474*

Blackburn

The largest town in East Lancashire, Blackburn is notable for its modern shopping malls, its celebrated three day market, its modern cathedral, and Thwaites Brewery, one of the biggest independent brewers of real ale in the north of England. Hard though it may be to imagine today, at the height of the textile industry, Blackburn was the biggest weaving town in the world. In 1931, it received arguably its most influential visitor when Mahatma Gandhi toured the area on a study trip of Lancashire's textile manufacture. Examples of the early machines, including James Hargreaves' Spinning Jenny and his carding machine, invented in 1760, can be seen at the *Lewis Textile Museum*, which is dedicated to the industry. The town's *Museum and Art Gallery* has, amongst its treasures, several paintings by Turner, the Hart collection of medieval manuscripts, and the finest collection of Eastern European icons in Britain.

Mentioned in the Domesday Book, the town was originally an agricultural community before the production of first woollen and then cotton cloth took over. Much of the town seen today was built on the prosperity brought by the cotton trade and, on the dome of St John's Church, can be seen a weathervane in the shape of a weaving shuttle. However, the town's prominence as a centre for the surrounding community has not been lost as, in 1926, the Diocese of Blackburn was created and the Gothic St Mary's Church, built in 1826, became the *Cathedral* of the Bishop of Blackburn.

Although Blackburn no longer has a manor house, Witton House has long since been demolished, the grounds have been turned into an excellent local amenity. *Witton Country Park* contains nature trails through woodlands up on to heather covered hill tops, all that remains of Witton House's once extensive grouse shoots.

South and West of Blackburn

Hoghton   *Map 2 ref F9*
4 miles W of Blackburn on A675
Originally a collection of hamlets with handloom weavers' cottages, the village was, during the 17th century, a place of unlawful Catholicism. *Arrowsmith House* was the place where Edmund Arrowsmith said his last mass before being captured and sentenced to death for being a Catholic priest and a Jesuit.

It is however, today, best known as the home of Lancashire's only true baronial residence *Hoghton Tower* which dates from 1565. The de Hoghton family have owned the land in this area since the time of the Norman Conquest and the house was built in a style in keeping with their social position and importance. The famous banqueting hall, on the ground floor, is where James I is said to have knighted the Sir Loin of Beef in 1617. The name of the house is though a little misleading as the tower was blown up by Cromwell's troops in 1643 when they over ran the Royalist garrison stationed here. Another famous visitor, who caused less disruption, was William Shakespeare who came to perform with William Hoghton's troupe of players. As well as the famous banqueting hall, other rooms open to the public include the beautifully preserved ballroom, the King's bedchamber, and the audience chamber. The grounds, too, are well worth a visit and are as perfectly preserved as the house.

Brindle
Map 2 ref E9

5 miles SW of Blackburn on B6256

An ancient village itself, Brindle's **St James' Church** celebrated its 800 year anniversary in 1990. Originally dedicated to St Helen, the patron saint of wells, the village probably grew up around a clean, fresh water supply, either from a well or spring.

Withnell Fold
Map 2 ref F9

5 miles SW of Blackburn off A674

Although this village is only a short and pleasant walk, crossing the Leeds and Liverpool Canal, from its neighbour Brindle, it is a very different place indeed. An industrial village, dominate by a huge chimney, Withnell Fold does, however, have its own claim to fame. The mill, built in 1844 overlooking the canal, became the world's biggest exporter of high-quality bank note paper.

Tockholes
Map 2 ref F9

3 miles SW of Blackburn off A666

This interesting, textile village was once an isolated centre of non-conformism and, next to a row of cottages, can be found the **United Reformed Chapel**, founded in 1662, though it has been rebuilt twice, in 1710 and in 1880. The **Parish Church** also has some unusual features and as well as the unique lance-shaped windows, there is an outdoor pulpit dating from the days when the whole congregation could not fit inside the building. Close to the pulpit is the grave of John Osbaldeston, the inventor of the weft fork, a gadget that allowed power looms to weave intricate patterns.

Just to the south of the village lies **Roddlesworth Nature Trail**, a path that follows the line of an old coach drive. Along the trail, for which details can be obtained at the information centre, can be found the ruins of **Hollinshead Hall**. Built in the 18th century and once very grand, the ruins were tidied up in the early 1990s but, fortunately, the wishing well has withstood the ravishes of time and neglect. Reminiscent of a small Georgian chapel, the well inside dates back to medieval times when its waters were thought to cure eye complaints.

The Victoria Hotel, in the centre of this quiet village, is a charming freehouse pub that is housed in an old cotton mill which dates from 1780. Previously called The Well Known Victoria Hotel, the pub has been owned and personally run by Jane and George Levey since the end of 1997 and they certainly have made this one of the best places for food and drink in the area. In attractive, comfort-

The Victoria Hotel

able surroundings, with plenty of old photographs of the village decorating the walls, visitors can enjoy a wide range of real ales, beers, and lagers as well as wine from the extensive list both by the bottle and also by the glass. The Victoria Hotel, however, is particularly popular with those who enjoy a delicious meal and Irene Carter, the chef, has put together an interesting menu that is sure to tempt everyone. The cosy restaurant is open every day except Mondays and, at the weekend, it is essential to book a table to avoid disappointment. As with many old buildings, the premises are said to be haunted and there have been many strange happenings taking place here over the years, though those of a nervous disposition should bear in mind that, so far, nothing sinister has taken place. *The Victoria Hotel, Golden Soney, Tockholes, Lancashire BB3 0NL Tel: 01254 701622*

Darwen
Map 2 ref G9

3 miles S of Blackburn on A666

Visitors to the town may be forgiven for thinking they have been here before as Darwen will be familiar to all viewers of the BBC series *Hetty Wainthropp Investigates,* which stars Patricia Routledge. Dominating the town from the west and situated high on Darwen Moor, is **Darwen Tower**, built to commemorate the Diamond Jubilee of Queen Victoria in 1897. The view from the top of the tower, which is always open, is enhanced by the height of the hill on which it stands (1,225 feet) and with the help of the plaques at the top much of the Lancashire landscape, and beyond, can be seen.

A striking landmark, very visible from the tower, and in the heart of Darwen is the chimney of the **India Mill**. Constructed out of hand-made bricks, it was built to resemble the campanile in St Mark's Square, Venice.

Darwen Tower

To the west of Darwen lies **Sunnyhurst Wood** and visitor centre in the valley of a gentle brook that originates on Darwen Moor to the south. Acquired by public subscription in 1902, to commemorate the coronation of Edward VII, this area of woodland, covering some 85 acres, is rich in both bird and plant life. The visitor centre, housed in an old keeper's cottage, has an ever changing exhibition and there is also the Olde England Kiosk, built in 1912, which serves all manner of refreshments.

Found in the heart of Darwen, in a pedestrian only area, ***Buxton's Coffee Shop and Bakery*** is the ideal place to take a break whilst out shopping and enjoy some freshly prepared refreshment. There has been a bakery here since 1896 and, since 1981, Buxton's has been in the capable hands of the Buxton family. Keith and son Ian are the bakers whilst daughter, Jackie, looks after the confectionery, and daughter-in-law, Denise, runs the shop. To ensure that the

Buxton's Coffee Shop and BAkery

business runs like a well-oiled machine, Connie, Keith's wife, oversees them all. The cosy coffee shop, adjacent to the bakery premises, is open from Monday to Saturday, during the day, and there is a full range of mouth-watering sandwiches, pies, home-made soups as well as wonderful cakes, sponges, and other sweet fancies. Many of the recipes used in the bakery, and then appearing in the coffee shop, have been handed down from the beginning of the century and there are many traditional favourites amongst them. *Buxton's Coffee Shop and Bakery, 15-17 Bridge Street, Darwen, Lancashire BB3 2AA Tel: 01254 702644 Fax: 01254 777513*

Little Darwen

Map 3 ref G9

3 miles S of Blackburn off A666

Found just to the north, at Little Darwen and dating back to the early 18th century, ***The Hindle Arms*** was originally built as a private dwelling for the local, wealthy Hindle family. The house, however, became a coaching inn and, towards the end of the 19th century, it became a fully licensed premises. Today, the inn is managed by Lisa and Mark who, though they have only been here since

The Hindle Arms

May 1998, have put a lot of work into turning around the fortunes of the pub. A warm and friendly couple, their enthusiasm along with the pleasant and comfortable surroundings have made this, once again, a popular place to visit. At the moment, though no food is served, an excellent range of real ales and beers are available behind the bar. For customers' entertainment, live music is played here from Thursday to Sunday evenings and there is also a separate games room. At the side of the pub there is also an attractive beer garden that is well used during the summer. Lisa and Mark plan to open up the functions room as a dining area and to begin to served meals shortly. *The Hindle Arms, 18 Raikes Bridge, Lower Darwen, Lancashire BB3 0HQ Tel: 01254 279239*

CHAPTER FIVE
West Lancashire

Wigan Pier

Chapter 5 - Area Covered

For precise location of places please refer to the colour maps found at the rear of the book.

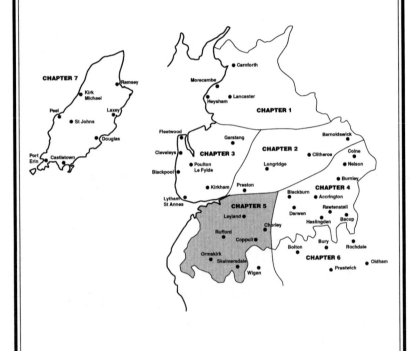

5
West Lancashire

Introduction

This area of Lancashire, with its sandy coastline and flat fertile farmland, is home to the elegant Victorian seaside resort of Southport, the ancient market towns of Chorley and Ormskirk, and Wigan, another ancient place with a rich industrial past. Following the reorganisation of the county boundaries in the 1970s and the creation of Merseyside, much of the coast and the southwestern area of Lancashire became part of the new county but the individual character and charm of this area has certainly not been lost.

As well as offering a step back in time, the broad promenades of Southport, its elegant tree-lined streets, and its superb shopping still makes this one of the most visited towns in this region. Though the silting up of the Ribble estuary, to the north, has caused the sea at this resort to recede, further south, at Ainsdale and Formby, not only is there paddling but also an vast expanse of sand dune and pine forest that is now an important nature reserve.

Behind the coast, the flat lands of the West Lancashire plain were once under water. Now with an extensive network of ditches, drainage has provided the old towns and quaint villages with rich fertile land that now produces a wealth of produce all year round and the roadside farm shops are very much a feature of the area.

Although there are several rivers flowing across the land, the chief water way, which is hard to miss, is the Leeds to Liverpool Canal. Linking the port of Liverpool with industrial Leeds and the many textile villages and towns in between, this major navigation changed the lives of many of the people living along its length.

Leeds and Liverpool Canal

However, the section through West Lancashire, passing rural villages, is perhaps one of the more pleasant stretches. There are plenty of charming canal side pubs in the area and walks along the towpath, through the unspoilt countryside, have been popular for many years. There is also, in this section, the wharf at Wigan Pier now a fascinating living museum that brings the canal to life.

Chorley

A bustling and friendly place, Chorley is a charming town that is locally famous for its market that dates back to 1498. Today, there are two markets - the covered market and the open, 'flat iron' market. This peculiar and intriguing name stems from the ancient practice of trading by displaying goods on the grounds without the use of stalls.

Dating back to 1360 and standing on the site of a Saxon chapel, the **Church of St Lawrence** is the town's oldest building. The church is said to contain the remains of St Lawrence, brought back from Normandy by Sir Richard Standish, and whether they are his relics or not, during the Middle Ages, the saint's shrine certainly brought pilgrims to the parish.

The Civil War also brought visitors to the town only less welcome ones. Following defeat at the nearby Battle of Preston, Royalist troops were twice engaged in battle here by Cromwell's victorious forces. Though not a happy time for both the Royalist and the town, the skirmishes did place Chorley on the historical map of England.

Chorley too was the birthplace, in 1819, of Henry Tate. The son of a Unitarian minister, in 1832, Henry was apprenticed to the grocery trade in Liverpool and, by 1855, he had not only set up his own business but also opened a chain of six shops. Selling the shops, Henry entered into the world of the competitive sugar trade and founded the world famous business of *Tate and Lyle*. Opening a new sugar refinery with the latest machinery from France, Henry cornered the refining business in Britain from which he made his fortune. A great benefactor, Henry not only gave away vast sums of money to worthy causes but also to the art gallery which now bears his name.

However, the jewel in Chorley's crown is, undoubtedly, *Astley Hall*. Built in the late 16th century and set within some beautiful parkland, the hall is a fine example of an Elizabethan mansion. Extended in 1666, and later in 1825, this is truly a house of history and the rooms, which reflect the passing of the centuries, contain superb items of furniture from 1600 to the Edwardian period. Whether or not Cromwell stayed at the hall following the Battle of Preston is open to debate but his boots are here on display.

The hall was given to the borough in 1922 by Reginald Tatton and it was he who insisted that the building should incorporate a memorial to those who had died in World War I. As a result, a small room has been devoted to the local men who fought and died for their country and, along with the display of photographs, there is a Book of Remembrance.

North of Chorley

Leyland   *Map 1 ref E9*
4 miles NW of Chorley on B5253

The town is probably best known for its associations with the manufacture of cars and lorries and the **British Commercial Vehicle Museum**, the largest such museum in Europe, is well worth a visit. Housed on the site of the former Leyland South Works, where commercial vehicles were produced for many years, there are many restored vans and lorries on display with exhibits ranging from the horsedrawn era, through steam-powered wagons right up to the present day vans and lorries.

Leyland is, however, an ancient settlement and documentary evidence has been found which suggests that the town was a Crown possession in Saxon times owned by Edward the Confessor. The village cross marks the centre of the old settlement, around which the town expanded and it is in this area of Leyland that the older buildings can be seen. Founded in the 11th century, much of the present **St Andrew's Church** dates from 1220 although there was some restoration work undertaken in the 15th century. The Eagle and Child Inn is almost as old, said to date from around 1230, and it served the needs of travellers journeying along the ancient highway which passed through the town.

Whilst not one of the town's oldest buildings, the old Grammar School, parts of which dates from the late 16th century, is hardly modern. Today it is home to the town's **Heritage Museum**, a fascinating place that describes, through interesting displays and exhibits, the history of this ancient market town.

Higher Penwortham   *Map 1 ref D8*
8 miles NW of Chorley on A59

Situated on Penwortham hill and overlooking the River Ribble, **St Mary's Church** has a 14th century chancel and a splendid tower. It stands on the site where the Romans are known to have had a building - probably a fort protecting the river.

Tarleton   *Map 1 ref D10*
8 miles W of Chorley off A59

This pleasant rural village, now by passed by the main road to Preston, is home to **St Mary's Church**, one of the finest buildings in Lancashire. Built in 1719, it is constructed from brick except for the cut-stone belfry. No longer the village church, it was replaced in the late 19th century by a larger building, it is still maintained and its churchyard has remained in use.

Croston   *Map 1 ref D10*
6 miles W of Chorley on A581

This historic village in the heart of rural West Lancashire, has been a centre for local farmers since it was granted a weekly market charter in 1283. Beside the banks of the River Yarrow, a tributary of the River Douglas, much of the village, including the 17th century almshouses and the lovely 15th century church, are part of a conservation area. The strong links with agriculture are still apparent in this area and the open farmland actually extends right into the village centre.

Ormskirk

The origins of this important market town on the West Lancashire plain date back to the time of the Vikings, when their leader, Orme, first settled the area in AD 840. The town received its first market charter from Edward I in 1286 and today, this is still a key event in the region. The partial drainage of Martin Mere, in the late 18th century, to provide more rich, fertile agricultural land, as well as the growth of nearby Liverpool, increased the prosperity of the town. Ormskirk was also touched by the Industrial Revolution and, whilst the traditional farming activities continued, cotton spinning and silk weaving also became important sources of local income. Today, the town has reverted to its traditional past.

The *Church of St Peter and St Paul*, in the centre of the town, unusually has both a steeple and a tower. The tower, added in the 16th century, was constructed to take the bells of Burscough Priory after the religious community had been disbanded by Henry VIII. However, the oldest feature found in the church is a stone carving on the outer face of the chancel's east wall that was probably the work of Saxon craftsmen.

Ormskirk too has a famous son: a market trader, called Beecham, who sold his own brand of liver pills that customers' described as 'worth a guinea a box'. His pills and powders made Beecham's fortune although his son, Thomas, a musical genius, brought world-wide fame to the family.

Just northeast of Ormskirk and situated on the site of 12th century Burscough Priory is *Abbey Farm Caravan Park*, the perfect place for a family holiday. The six acre site has space for 65 touring caravans that are offered either hard or soft standing in pitches that have been made secluded and private with the help of mature trees and shrubbery. Es-

Abbey Farm Caravan Park

tablished for over 25 years, the site has been owned and personally run by Joan and Alan Bridge since the late 1980s and, as well as offering all the usual modern day amenities, this is a friendly and well-maintained park. Both children and pets are welcome and there is a large recreational field, complete with a safe adventure playground, that will keep the children amused. Although Abbey Farm Caravan Park has a quiet, rural setting, it is ideally placed for the many attractions of Lancashire. *Abbey Farm Caravan Park, Dark Lane, Ormskirk, Lancashire L40 5TX Tel & Fax: 01695 572686*

North of Ormskirk

Burscough   *Map 1 ref D11*
2 miles NE of Ormskirk on A59
Situated on the banks of the Leeds and Liverpool Canal, the village's Parish Church was one of the Million, or Waterloo, Churches built as a thanks to God after the final defeat of Napoleon in 1815. A later addition to the church is the Memorial Window to those of the parish who died for their country during the First World War.

Little remains of **Burscough Priory**, founded in the early 12th century by the Black Canons. Receiving lavish endowments from the local inhabitants, the priory was, at one time, one of the most influential religious houses in Lancashire.

Rufford   *Map 1 ref D10*
5 miles NE of Ormskirk on B5246
This attractive village of pretty houses is notable for its church and its beautiful old hall. Built in 1869, the church is a splendid example of the Gothic revival period and its tall spire dominates the skyline.

The ancestral home of the Hesketh family who were involved in reclaiming the mosslands on their estates, **Rufford Old Hall** is without a doubt one of the finest 15th century buildings in the county. Particularly noted for its magnificent Great Hall, this impressive black and white timbered house is well worth exploring. From the superb, intricately carved movable wooden screen to the solid oak chests and long refectory table, the atmosphere here is definitely one of wealth and position.

Now in the hands of the National Trust, within the outbuildings there is not only a shop and a popular restaurant but also the **Philip Ashcroft Museum of Rural Life**, with its unique collection of items that illustrate fully village life in pre-industrial Lancashire.

Rufford Old Hall

Mere Brow *Map 1 ref C10*

7 miles N of Ormskirk on B5246

Just to the south of the village lies the Wildfowl and Wetlands Trust at **Martin Mere**, over 350 acres of reclaimed marshland which was established in 1976 as a refuge for thousands of wintering wildfowl. Until Martin Mere was drained in the 17th century, to provide rich, fertile farmland, the lake was one of the largest in England. Indeed, some believe that it was into Martin Mere that King Arthur's sword, Excalibur, was tossed after the king's death.

Today, the stretches of water, mudbanks, and grassland provide homes for many species of birds and, with a network of hides, visitors can observe the birds in their natural habitats. There are also a series of pens, near to the visitors centre, where many other birds can be seen all year round at closer quarters. Particularly famous for the vast numbers pink-footed geese which winter here, their number often approaching 20,000, although winter is a busy time at Martin Mere, a visit in any season is sure to be rewarded. The visitor centre caters for everyone and, as well as the shop and café, there is a theatre and a wealth of information regarding the birds found here and the work of the Trust.

The charming **Legh Arms**, in the heart of this quiet rural village, dateing back some 150 years was originally built as a farmhouse. Open every day, and all day at the weekends, this attractive pub is hard to miss as, during the summer, it is bedecked

The Legh Arms

with colourful hanging baskets and flower filled tubs. This glorious display, put on by landlord and lady, Ray and Barbara Andrew, is as bright and cheerful as the welcome all who come here receive from the couple. Popular locally for its excellent range of real ales and delicious, home-cooked menu, The Legh Arms is everything a country pub should be. An excellent place for the whole family, the rear beer garden is as attractive and well-maintained as the rest of the pub and this is certainly a place not to be missed. *The Legh Arms, 82 The Gravel, Mere Brow, near Tarleton, Lancashire PR4 6JX Tel: 01772 814378*

Churchtown   Map 1 ref C10
7 miles NW of Ormskirk on A5267

This charming village, now a small part of Southport, has retained much of its village feel and is certainly worthy of exploration in its own right. Considerably predating the seaside resort, Churchtown is, as its name suggests, centred around its church. Dedicated to St Cuthbert, it is possible that whilst fleeing from the Danes, the monks of Lindisfarne rested here with the relics of their famous saint.

However, it is likely that the village was, for many years, known by the name of North Meols and a chapel of Mele was mentioned in the Domesday Book. Derived from the Norse word 'melr' meaning sand dune, there was certainly a thriving fishing village here in the early 12th century. In 1224, Robert de Coudrey granted the village the right to hold a market, the likely place for which is the cross standing opposite the church in the heart of the village.

As the settlement lay on a crossroads and at the start of a route over the sands of the Ribble estuary, it was a place of considerable importance. It was also here that the tradition of sea bathing in this area began, when, in 1219 St Cuthbert's Eve was declared a fair day, which later became known as Bathing Sunday.

There is still plenty to see in this small village. The present **Meols Hall** dates from the 17th century but its appearance today is largely thanks to the work carried out by the late Colonel Roger Fleetwood Hesketh in the 1960s. When the colonel took over the house in the late 1930s, the older and larger part of the hall had been demolished in 1733 and the remaining building was rather nondescript. Taking the gabled bay of the late 17th century, extensions were added to give the house a varied roofline and a three dimensional frontage.

The hall is the last home of the Hesketh family, who, at one time, had owned most of the coastal area between Southport and Heysham. Originally, the manor had been granted to Robert de Coudrey, coming into the Hesketh family by marriage in the late 16th century, and there has been a house on this site since the 13th century. Occasionally open to visitors, the hall has a fine art collection and, in the entrance hall, are three carved chairs that were used in Westminster Abbey for the coronation of Charles II. During World War I, Moels Hall was used as a military hospital.

Planned on the site of the old Churchtown Strawberry Gardens in 1874, the **Botanic Gardens**, restored in 1937, are beautifully maintained and present a superb example of classic Victorian garden design. With magnificent floral displays, a boating lake, wide, twisting paths, and a fernery, little has changed here since the day the gardens were first opened by the Rev Charles Hesketh. Built in 1938, following the gardens' restoration, the **Botanic Bowling Pavilion** mimics the style of the late Regency architect Decimus Burton. Here too is the **Botanic Gardens Museum**, with its fine exhibition on local history and its gallery of Victoriana.

Southport   Map 1 ref B10
8 miles NW of Ormskirk on A570

The rise of this popular and still elegant Victorian seaside resort lies in the tradition of sea bathing that began at nearby Churchtown centuries ago. As the number of people celebrating Bathing Sunday grew, the need for a more accessible beach also grew and a stretch of sand two miles south of Churchtown was deemed suitable. As the crowds flocked over the sand dunes the need for accommodation increased and a local entrepreneur, known as Duke Sutton, built the first hotel of driftwood in 1792. It was Doctor Barton who, when christening Sutton's hotel with a bottle of champagne, coined the name Southport (the South Port Hotel) and the town grew up around the ramshackle building.

The driftwood hotel was replaced by a grander stone building, known as the Duke's Folly as its construction resulted in Sutton losing all his money and being imprisoned in Lancaster jail in 1803. Now an established town, the expansion of Southport came as a result, as with all of the region's famous resorts, of the extension of the railway services from the mill towns of Lancashire and from Manchester and Liverpool. Of all these places, none has managed to retain is air of Victorian grandeur more so than Southport.

The town's central, main boulevard, **Lord Street**, is a mile long wide road that was built along the boundary bordering the lands of the two neighbouring lords of the manor. A superb shopping street today, the exceptionally wide pavements, with gardens along one side and an elegant glass-topped canopy along most of the other side, make this one of the most pleasant places to shop in the country. Many of the town's classical style buildings are found along its length and it has been designated a conservation area. Off Lord Street, there is one of the town's several covered arcades and, built in 1898, **Wayfarers Arcade** is one of the best. The modest

Lord Street, Southport

entrance opens out into a beautiful cast iron and glass conservatory, with its first floor gallery and splendid central dome. Originally named the Leyland Arcade after the town's Member of Parliament, it took its present name in 1976 after the arcade's most successful leaseholder.

In a central position along Lord Street lies Southport's rather modest **Town Hall**. Built in 1852 and of a classical design, above the balcony is a beautiful carving in bold relief of the figures of Justice, Mercy, and Truth picked out in white against a Wedgwood blue background. Further along, the Atkinson Central Library was built in 1879 as the premises of the Southport and West Lancashire Bank. The original ceiling of the banking hall can still be seen as can its fireplace. On the first floor is the **Atkinson Art Gallery** which contains collections of British art and Chinese porcelain.

However, not all the buildings in Southport are Victorian and the **Top Rank Bingo Club**, originally called the Garrick Theatre, was held to be the finest theatre when it was opened in 1932. With much of its exterior as it would have appeared when it first opened, it is a wonderful example of the Art Deco style. Finally, Lord Street is also home to the town's war memorial, **The Monument**. Opened on Remembrance Day, 1923 by the Earl of Derby, this is a large and grand memorial that remains the town's focal point. Its design was the subject of a competition and the winning entry was submitted by Garyson and Barnish, the designers of the famous Royal Liver Building in Liverpool. The central obelisk is flanked by twin colonnades in which the names of the town's over 1,000 dead are inscribed.

As every Victorian resort had a **Promenade**, so does Southport and this is a typical example: flanked by grand hotels on the land side and a series of formal gardens on the other. As the silting up of the Ribble estuary progressed unchecked the **Marine Lake** was constructed at the northern end of the promenade. At over 86 acres, this man-made lake is the largest in Britain and, as well as being an attractive site and a place for the pursuit of all manner of watersports, it is also host to an annual 24-hour yacht race.

From the centre of the promenade extends Southport's **Pier** which, at 1,460 yards long, was the longest pier in the country until 1897. Following a fire in 1933 it was shortened but it remains the second longest in the country. Looking at the pier today it is hard to imagine that at the end of the last century pleasure steamers were able to depart from here to Barrow in Cumbria, Bangor, Wales, and the Isle of Man. Along the shore line, and opened in the spring of 1998, the new sea wall and **Marine Drive** is a wonderful modern construction, the length of Southport's sea front, that blends well with the town's Victorian heritage.

The normal attractions of a seaside resort have not been forgotten and **Pleasureland** is the obvious choice for those seeking thrills and hair-raising rides. Keen gardeners will know of Southport for its splendid annual Flower Show, second only to Chelsea, and golfers will be familiar with the name of Royal Birkdale Golf Course, just south of the town centre. Southport has one more sporting association of which it is justly proud. From behind a car show room in the 1970s, Ginger McCain trained Red Rum on the sands of Southport to a record breaking three magnificent wins in the Grand National run at Aintree. A statue of the great horse can be seen in Wayfarers Aracade.

Scarisbrick   *Map 1 ref C11*
3 miles N of Ormskirk on A570

The village, which is the largest parish in Lancashire, lies in the heart of rich agricultural land that is intensively cultivated for vegetables, including carrots, brussel sprouts, cabbages, and early potatoes. A feature of this area are the large number of farm shops, by the side of the road, selling the produce fresh from the fields.

The first *Scarisbrick Hall* was built in the reign of King Stephen but, in the middle of the 19th century, the hall, which is screened from the road by thick woodland, was extensively remodelled by the Victorian architect Augustus Welby Pugin for Charles Scarisbrick. In 1945, the hall and surrounding extensive grounds were sold by the last member of the family to live here, Sir Everard Scarisbrick, and today it remains an independent boarding school.

South and West of Ormskirk

Halsall   *Map 1 ref C11*
4 miles W of Ormskirk on A5147

This is a charming unspoilt village lying in the heart of fertile West Lancashire and close to the Leeds and Liverpool Canal - the longest canal in Britain with a mainline of 127.25 miles and 92 locks plain. *St Cuthbert's Church*, which dates from the middle of the 13th century, is one of the oldest churches in the diocese of Liverpool and it remains one of the prettiest in the county. The spire, which was added in the 15th century, rises from a tower that has octagonal upper stages.

Haskayne   *Map 1 ref C11*
4 miles W of Ormskirk on A5147

Situated just to the south of Halsall, in the village of Haskayne, and on the banks of the Leeds and Liverpool Canal, *The Ship Inn* is a hidden place that is well worth finding. Originally built in 1787 for a barge owner, this was the first inn opened along the banks of the canal, and today it remains one of the most pleasantly located pubs

The Ship Inn

in Lancashire. However, it is not just for its perfect position that the pub is popular but also for the excellent hospitality offered by hosts Susan and Kevin Stephenson. As well as serving a range of real ales, beers, lagers, and ciders, The Ship Inn has an appetising menu of tasty meals and snacks that are served for lunch and dinner during the week and all day at weekends. Children too are not forgotten, it should be remembered that this was the first pub in Lancashire to have a family room, and there is an imaginative and safe play area for them outside. Adults can also enjoy the fresh air, taking their food and drink into the attractive beer garden, overlooking the canal. *The Ship Inn, 6 Rosemary Lane, Haskayne, Lancashire L39 7JP Tel: 01704 840572*

Ainsdale
Map 1 ref B11

7 miles W of Ormskirk on A565

Towards the sea, from the centre of the village, lies what was Ainsdale-on-Sea with its old Lido and the more modern Pontin's holiday village. Between here and Formby, further down the coast, the sand dunes form part of the ***Ainsdale National Nature Reserve*** and one of the most extensive dune systems in the country. Breeding in the shallow pools that form in the sand dunes, this is one of the last homes of the endangered natterjack toad. As well as supporting the toads, the salt pools are the natural habitat for a variety of dune plants, including dune helleborine, grass of Parnassus and round-leaved wintergreen.

Formby
Map 1 ref B11
8 miles W of Ormskirk off A565

The origins of this small coastal town lie in the time of the Vikings and the name Formby comes from the Norse *Fornebei* meaning Forni's town. Between the Norman Conquest and the time of the Dissolution in 1536, there were a succession of landowners but, by the mid-16th century, the Formby and Blundell families emerged as the chief owners. **Formby Hall**, built for William Formby in 1523, occupies a site that was first developed in the 12th century.

Today, Formby is perhaps better known as a quiet and desirable residential area and also the home of an important red squirrel sanctuary at the National Trust **Freshfield Nature Reserve** and pine forest. Linked with Ainsdale's nature reserve, the two form over 400 acres of dunes and woodland, as well as shoreline, from which there are magnificent views over the Mersey estuary and, on a clear day, the hills of Wales and of Lakeland are also visible.

Great Altcar
Map 1 ref B11
6 miles W of Ormskirk on B5195

Standing on the banks of the River Alt, this old farming village is famous as the venue for the Liverpool Cup, an annual hare coarsing event. In the churchyard of the present church, erected by the Earl of Sefton in 1879, are a pedestal font and a stoup which came from the earlier churches that occupied this site.

Ince Blundell
Map 1 ref B12
6 miles W of Ormskirk off A565

The village takes part of its name from the Blundell family who have, for centuries, exerted much influence on the village and surrounding area. Ince comes from the Celtic word 'Ynes' which means an island within a watery meadow and it would have perfectly described the village's situation before the surrounding land was drained.

The annual candlelight service at the village **Church of the Holy Family** is an ancient custom that appears to be unique to this country. The people of the parish decorate the graves in the cemetery with flowers and candles before holding a service there. Common in Belgium, this custom was brought to the village at the beginning of the 20th century.

Sefton
Map 1 ref C12
6 miles SW of Ormskirk on B5422

This quiet old village lies on the edge of a rich and fertile plain of farmland that lies just behind the West Lancashire coast. Part of the estate of the Earls of Sefton (descendents of the Molyneux family) up until 1972, the 16th century village **Church** has several monuments to the family as well as a 14th century spire. Though this is a small village, its name has also been given to the large metropolitan district of north Merseyside which stretches from Bootle to Southport.

Lydiate
Map 1 ref C12
4 miles SW of Ormskirk on A5147

This is another pleasant, old village bordering the flat open farmland created from the West Lancashire mosses. Lydiate itself means an enclosure with a gate to stop cattle roaming and, though the age of the settlement here is uncertain, the now ruined **St Katharine's Chapel** dates from the 15th century. However, the most frequented building in the village is **The Scotch Piper**, a lovely cruck-framed house with a thatched roof that has the reputation for being the oldest pub in Lancashire.

Aughton
Map 1 ref C12
3 miles SW of Ormskirk off A59

This picturesque village, surrounded by agricultural land, is dominated by the spire of **St Michael's Church**. An ancient place, it was mentioned in the Domesday Book, the register of church rectors goes back to 1246 and much of the building's medieval framework remains though its was restored in 1914.

Close by lies the **Old Hall** which stands on a site that has been occupied since Saxon times. The ruins of a 15th century pele tower are visible in the garden and, as well as having a priest's hole, the house is reputed to have been Cromwell's base whilst he was active in the area.

Found opposite St Michael's Church is **The Stanley Arms**, a former coaching inn that dates back to the early 18th century which was, during the 19th century, a post house. As befits a building of this age, the pub is reputed to have a ghost though the landlord and lady, Steven and Sandra, have yet to make its acquaintance. This is a truly charming pub, set in a tranquil and peaceful position, that is well worth seeking out. There is a pleasant garden area as well as a safe children's play area for fine days whilst, inside, the pub is cosy and welcoming. Popular for its fine array of real ales, The Stanley Arms is also gaining a reputation for the delicious menu of reasonably priced, home-made dishes that make a change from the more usual pub food. A cracking place, with warm and friendly

The Stanley Arms

staff, those who enjoy live music should note that every other Friday night features an act, whilst there is a quiz every Tuesday evening open to everyone. *The Stanley Arms, St Michael Road, Aughton, near Ormskirk, Lancashire L39 6SA Tel: 01695 423241*

East of Ormskirk

Westhead   Map 1 ref D11

1 mile E of Ormskirk on A577

At Westhead, just to the east of Ormskirk, and dating back to the late 19th century, the **Halton Castle** pub sits right on the main road through the village and this striking black and white building is hard to miss. Well decorated and comfortably furnished, the various areas which make up the interior of the pub are aptly named The Keep, The Moat, and The Dungeon. The stylish dining area is particularly welcoming with its feature fireplace and stained glass windows. Although the hosts, Carol and Billy Quirk, have only been at Halton Castle since spring 1998, they have certainly made their mark and the pleasant, friendly atmosphere and excellent hospitality is down to them and their charming staff. As well as serving a fine range of Burtonwood ales, there are all the usual beers, lagers, and ciders and the pub also has an extensive menu of tasty dishes, from juicy sandwiches to three course Sunday lunches, that prove very popular. For customers' entertainment there is a live show on

The Halton Castle

Saturday evenings and, to the rear of the pub, is a superb bowling green. *Halton Castle, 1 Cross Hall Brow, Westhead, near Ormskirk, Lancashire L40 6JF Tel: 01695 573596*

Lathom   *Map 1 ref D11*
3 miles NE of Ormskirk off A5209

The stretch of the famous Leeds and Liverpool Canal which passes through this village is well worth a visit and it includes the **Top Locks** area, a particularly interesting part of this major canal route.

The Ring O'Bells is an attractive red brick pub standing adjacent to the Leeds and Liverpool Canal in the centre of the village. Managed by Lillian and Barry Murphy, this is a popular local inn

The Ring O'Bells

that welcomes visitors, particularly those in search of a good pint of beer and a tasty meal. The bar serves all the usual ales, bitters, lagers, and ciders and, throughout the day, there is also an extensive menu of delicious meals and bar snacks that is supplemented by the daily specials board. Comfortable and well decorated inside, the addition of ceiling beams and a feature fireplace give the pub a real olde worlde atmosphere whilst the displays of brassware, bells, tankards, and other memorabilia add plenty of interest. *The Ring O'Bells, Ring O'Bells Lane, Lathom, Lancashire L40 5TE Tel: 01704 893157*

Parbold   *Map 1 ref D11*
5 miles E of Ormskirk off A5209

This is a charming village of pretty stone cottages as well as grand, late-Victorian houses built by wealthy Manchester cotton brokers. It is also home to **Parbold Hill**, one of the highest points for miles around and from which there are superb views of the West Lancashire plain. At the summit stands a rough hewn monument, erected to commemorate the Reform Act of 1832, that is locally known, due to its shape, as Parbold Bottle.

Ashurst Beacon, another local landmark, was re-erected on Ashurst Hill by Lord Skelmersdale in 1798 when the threat of a French invasion was thought to be imminent.

Mawdesley   *Map 1 ref D10*
6 miles NE of Ormskirk off B5246

This quiet village is well worth a visit as it is a past winner of the Best Kept Village of Lancashire award. Surrounded by the farmland of the West Lancashire plain, this rural village was once associated with a thriving basket making industry, founded 150 years ago. Mawdesley Hall, thought to have been erected by William Mawdesley in 1625, has some key architectural features and the village school is certainly worth a second glance.

Found in the centre of the village, opposite the Post Office, is the striking **Red Lion** pub which is hard to miss with its black and white frontage and colourful hanging baskets, window boxes, and tubs. Approximately 170 years old, the building was once used as the stables for the next door Co-op store and one of the outstanding features of the pub today is its enclosed Continental-style patio that the courtyard now holds. The pub has been owned by business partners, Stella Thompson and Edward Newton, since the summer of 1997 and, in that short time, they have really made their mark here as well as having undertaken some extensive renovation work.

The Red Lion

Well known for the excellent range of real ales, beers, and other drinks available at the bar, The Red Lion also has a fantastic menu that is both imaginative and extensive and fast gaining the pub an enviable reputation. To complete this picture of what must be one of the best pubs in the area, the interior is divided up into a series of rooms each with their own particular charm. The cosy Snug is the place to meet friends for a drink and a chat whilst the Lounge Bar is the haunt, on Sunday afternoons, of jazz fans and in the evening there is a mixture of live music to enjoy. Perhaps, however, the conservatory dining room is the most spectacular room of all, with its bright Mediterranean colours and solid pine furniture it is the ideal place to enjoy a delicious meal. *The Red Lion, New Street, Mawdesley, Lancashire L40 2QP Tel: 01704 822208/822999 Fax: 01704 822208*

Wrightington   Map 1 ref E11
8 miles NE of Ormskirk on B5250

By passed by most people as they travel up and down the nearby M6 and overshadowed by the delights of the **Camelot Theme Park** at nearby **Charnock Richard**, this is another pleasant, rural Lancashire village.

Conveniently situated in this quiet village, yet close to the M6 motorway, **The Tudor Inn** is a delightful place that is managed by a charming couple, Nora and Gerry Johnston. Visitors here could not be in better hands as the couple were not only voted Innkeeper of the Year for the Northwest in 1997 but also for the North and Scotland in 1996. So, though they have only been at The Tudor Inn

The Tudor Inn

since Easter 1998, customers will not be surprised to find that they have already made their mark here and turned the pub into a very popular place indeed.

Over the years these former cottages, with a smithy to the rear, were known as The White Lion Inn and, locally as Old Bobs, but, though the name has changed in the last 20 years, the excellent interior decoration, with plenty of olde worlde artefacts on display, still brings back an age of good hospitality. This is also what locals and visitors to the inn find today. As well as the superb range of ales and beers behind the bar, there is a full and comprehensive menu of delicious bar snacks and meals available every day at both lunchtime (except Monday) and in the evening. Both children and the disabled customer are equally well catered for and are welcome to join in the fun. *The Tudor Inn, 117 Mossy Lea Road, Wrightington, Lancashire WN6 9RE Tel: 01257 424143*

Rivington   Map 2 ref F10
13 miles E of Ormskirk off A673

This is a charming village surrounded by moorland of outstanding natural beauty that forms the western border of the Forest of Rossendale. Overlooking the village, and with splendid views over West Lancashire, **Rivington Pike**, at 1,191 feet, is one of the area's high spots. It was once a site of one of the country's chain of signal beacons.

Just to the south of the village lies **Lever Park**, situated on the lower slopes of Rivington Moor, which was made over to the public in 1902 by William Hesketh Lever, who later became Lord Leverhulme. The park comprises an awe-inspiring pot pourri of ornamental, landscaped gardens, tree-lined avenues, cruck-framed barns, a Georgian hall, and a treasure trove of natural history within its 2,000 acres. The park's moorland setting, elevated position, and adjoining reservoirs provide scenery on a grand scale which leaves a lasting impression.

Adlington   *Map 2 ref F10*
11 miles E of Ormskirk on A6

To the west of Rivington, at Adlington, and dating back to 1760, the attractive **Spinners Arms** in the heart of the town, was originally built as three cottages and, as the name suggests, it was also home to a once thriving cottage textile industry. Another of the three

The Spinners Arms

cottages is also known to have brewed its own beer and this was probably the beginnings of the pub as it is known today. Cosy and comfortable inside, this is just the place to come to relax and enjoy a pint of beer whilst catching up on the local news. The interior, which retains many Victorian features and a superb flagstone floor in the games rooms, is particularly pleasant and adds to the warm and friendly atmosphere of the inn. Open all day, every day, The Spinners Arms also has a range of tasty bar snacks available from noon until 18.00. *The Spinners Arms, 105 Railway Road, Adlington, near Chorley, Lancashire PR6 9QZ Tel: 01257 480113*

Standish
Map 1 ref E11

9 miles E of Ormskirk on A49

This historic old market town has several reminders to its past and not least of these is the splendid **St Wilfrid's Church**. Built in a size and style that befitted the importance of the town in the late 16th century, the building stands on the site of a church that was certainly here at the beginning of the 13th century. A look around the interior of the church will provide a potted history of the area: there are tombs and memorials to all the local families including the Wrightingtons, Shevingtons, and the Standish family themselves.

The Standish family came from Normandy and crossed the channel with William the Conqueror. One of the family members became the Warden of Scarborough Castle and another, Ralph de Standish, was knighted after his part in quelling the Peasants' Revolt. There was even a Standish at Agincourt. However, the most famous member of the family is Miles Standish who sailed to the New World on board the *Mayflower* with the Pilgrim Fathers in 1620. This may seem strange as the Standish family were staunch Catholics. Though there is little left in the way of monuments to the family in this country, their home (put up for sale in 1920 after the last family member died) was demolished and parts transported to America, Miles Standish is remembered in the town of Duxbury in America.

The Boar's Head Inn is one of the oldest drinking premises in the country, second only to the Trip to Jerusalem in Nottingham, and it dates back to 1271. Though it is now in a relatively tucked away position, the pub stood at the junction where the road to York and Durham met the road to Kendal, Carlisle, and Scotland. Though much, over the years, has been lost, there are several original features still remaining including the old cells, where prisoners convicted at Chester assizes were held for the night on their way to be hanged at Lancaster Castle, and the ancient ceiling beams.

Managed since 1995 by Di and Malc Meadows, The Boar's Head Inn has a lot to offer its customers. There is an excellent array of beers and ales at the bar as well as a choice of wines, some very popular fruit wines, and their home-made sangria. The food too, is fantastic and, served at lunchtime, it is well worth sampling. With a fast growing reputation, the delicious menu of home-made dishes draws people from near and far and it is necessary to book at the weekend. As well as this historic and atmospheric interior, there is a delightful beer garden, bedecked with a colourful mass of flowers that are a sight worth seeing in themselves.

The Boar's Head Inn

Finally, rugby fans might recognise Malc, as he was a player in both league and union before retiring to the licensing trade. *The Boar's Head Inn, Wigan Road, Standish, Lancashire WN6 0AD Tel: 01942 749747*

The outstanding *Charnley Arms* dates back some 150 years and, though it has had several names in the past, today, its name is a tribute to one of Standish's most prominent citizens, the late professor Sir John Charnley. A pioneering surgeon, it was Sir John who made nearby Wrightington Hospital an international centre of excellence in orthopaedic surgery. The tribute is indeed a fitting one as the pub changed its name to The Charnley Arms after a total refurbishment in 1993 which today makes this one of the most attractive and comfortable places in the area. Full of nooks and crannies, this large pub offers customers plenty of quiet, secluded seating and the mass of memorabilia and other ornaments add to the sense of age and to the atmosphere that is also created by the superb fireplaces.

This is an excellent place for all the family, where not only is there a well-stocked bar but also a comprehensive menu of interest-

The Charnley Arms

ing and tasty snacks and meals. Certainly not the usual run of the mill pub grub, a meal out here, with a cocktail before hand, will be an experience worth savouring and it will come as no surprise that The Charnley Arms is fast gaining an enviable reputation of which landlord and lady, Jeff and Julie Fletcher, can be justly proud. With superb facilities for children and the disabled guests, as well as the attractive, shrubbed beer garden, this is a place well worth seeking out. *The Charnley Arms, Almondbrook Road, Standish, Lancashire WN6 0SS Tel: 01257 424619*

Found just over a mile from the centre of Standish and opposite the original 13th century Seven Stars pub - now a private dwelling - is *The New Seven Stars* pub, which is itself around 140 years old. A striking black and white building that is hard to miss, the pub is

The New Seven Stars

managed by Jennie and Don who, in the time they have been here, have made this a very popular place with locals and visitors alike. Open all day, every day, during the summer, not only is there a fine selection of beers, ales, and lagers behind the bar but also a tasty menu of bar snacks and meals are served. This is also the place to come to for live music as, on Friday evenings, there is always a band and once a month, on Saturday night, The New Seven Stars holds a rock disco. For those who enjoy a quieter atmosphere but also some fun, there is a quiz each Sunday evening to which all are welcome. *The New Seven Stars, 489 Preston Road, Standish, Lancashire WN6 0QD Tel: 01257 421144*

Shevington
Map 1 ref E11
8 miles E of Ormskirk on B5375

In the centre of Shevington, a small village to the west of Standish lies **The Plough and Harrow**, a large Edwardian, red brick pub that has been run by Nick and Lauren du Toit since 1995. Nick was a professional Rugby league players first with Wigan and then mov-

The Plough and Harrow

ing to Wakefield and Barrow and, not surprisingly, there is plenty of sporting memorabilia decorating the interior. Open all day, every day, well-kept real ales are very much the order of the day in this well-frequented pub. Warm and friendly where no one stays a stranger for long, as well as the sporting theme, there is live music at the Plough and Harrow on Thursday and Saturday evenings. This must be Lauren's influence as she is a singer herself. *The Plough and Harrow, Broad Oth Lane, Shevington, near Wigan, Lancashire WN6 8EA Tel: 01257 252375*

Wigan
Map 2 ref E12

10 miles E of Wigan on A577

Although to many this town is a product of the industrial age, Wigan is one of the oldest places in Lancashire. As far back as the 1st century AD there was a Celtic Brigantes settlement here that was taken over by the Romans who built a small town called Coccium. Little remains of those far off days but, during the construction of a gasworks in the mid-19th century various burial urns were unearthed during the excavation work. The town's name comes from Wic-Ham which is probably Anglo-Saxon or Breton in origin but, following the departure of the Romans, the settlement lay in that part of the country that was forever fluctuating between the kingdoms of Mercia and Northumbria so the derivation is uncertain.

The medieval age brought more settled times and, by the end of the 13th century, the town had not only been granted a market charter but was also sending two members to Parliament. A staunchly Catholic town, Wigan fared badly during the Civil War. The Earl of Derby, whose home, Lathom House, lay on the outskirts of the town, was a favourite with the King and this was where Charles I made his base for his attacks on Roundhead Bolton. The bitter attacks on Wigan by the Cromwellian troops saw the fortifications destroyed and both the parish church and the moot hall were looted. The Battle of Wigan Lane, the last encounter between the warring forces in Lancashire, is commemorated by a monument which stands on the place where a key member of the Earl of Derby's forces was killed.

Wigan's development as an industrial town centred around coal mining, which began as early as 1450. By the 19th century, there were over 1,000 pit shafts in operation in the surrounding area, supplying the fuel for Lancashire's expanding textile industry. The Leeds and Liverpool Canal, which runs through the town, was a key means of transporting the coal to the cotton mills of Lancashire and **Wigan Pier**, the major loading bay, remains one of the most substantial and interesting features of the waterway. A well-known musical hall joke, first referred to by George Formby senior as he told of the virtues of his home town over Blackpool, it was the 1930s

Wigan Pier

novel by George Orwell, *The Road to Wigan Pier*, that really put the old wharf on the map. Today, the pier has been beautifully restored and it is now a key attraction in the area. There are canal boat rides and a superb exhibition, The Way We Were, based on local social history and with costumed actors playing the part of the townsfolk of the 19th century. The pier is also home to **Trencherfield Mill** where not only is there the largest working mill engine in the world on display but also a collection of old textile machines and other engines.

However, Wigan is not a town living in the past but, as well as having a modern town centre with all the usual amenities, there is some fine countryside on the doorstep, including the **Douglas Valley Trail**, along the banks of the River Douglas. Even the town's coal mining past has interesting links with the natural world: **Pennington Flash** is a large lake formed by mining subsidence that is now a wildlife reserve and a country park. To the north of the town lies **Haigh Country Park**, one of the first to be designated in England, that is formed from the estate of the Earls of Crawford. Although Haigh Hall is not open to the public, the park includes areas of mixed woodland as well as a children's play area and a café.

Westhoughton *Map 2 ref F11*
15 miles E of Ormskirk on A58

This small industrial town grew up around the development of Lancashire's coal mining industry in the late 18th and early 19th century.

The Rose and Crown is an attractive pub which dates back to the mid-19th century and it was owned for many years by the local brewery Magee Marshall. Today, the pub is managed by the very capable couple, Irene and Joe Williamson, who, in the 30 years that they have been here, have made the pub the popular place it is now. Very stylish inside, the walls display many of the items that Irene and Joe have collected over the years, including all manner of horse

The Rose and Crown

tack and a brilliant array of gleaming brassware. However, what really draws people to The Rose and Crown is the excellent beer and the regular entertainment. In fact, there is something on every evening except Mondays and the wide variety of tastes catered for is an indication of the care and attention that Irene and Joe pay to their customers' needs. As well as the Sunday night guitar jamming sessions and the Saturday evening live music, there are quiz nights, country bands, and line dancing. *The Rose and Crown, 220-222 Bolton Road, Westhoughton, Lancashire BL5 3EE Tel: 01942 790242*

CHAPTER SIX
East Lancashire

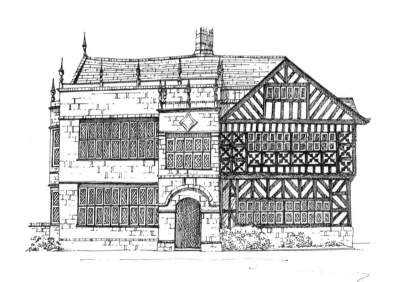

Hall-i'-th,-Wood

Chapter 6 - Area Covered

For precise location of places please refer to the colour maps found at the rear of the book.

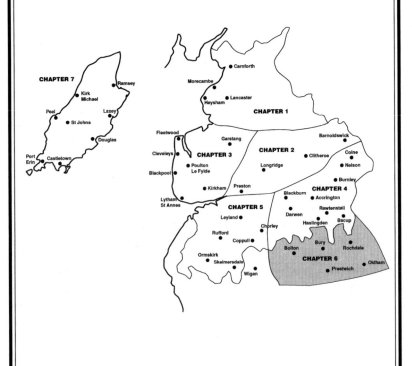

6
East Lancashire

Introduction

This area of the county, to the north of Manchester and west of the
Pennines, is, perhaps, everyone's idea of Lancashire. A region dominated by cotton, East Lancashire has risen and fallen with the
fluctuations in the trade over the years but, behind the dark, sa-
tanic mills is a population full of humour and wit as well as some
splendid countryside.

Before the Industrial Revolution this was a sparsely populated
region of remote hillside farms and cottages that relied, chiefly, on
sheep farming and the wool trade. Many of the settlements date
back to before the Norman Conquest and, though little may have
survived the rapid building of the 19th century, there are three surprisingly wonderful ancient houses to be seen here: Smithills Hall
and Hall-i'-th'-Wood at Bolton and Turton Tower, just to the north.

However, there is no escaping the textile industry. Lancashire's
ideal climate for cotton spinning and weaving - damp so that the
yarn does not break - made it the obvious choice for the building of
the mills. There are numerous valleys with fast flowing rivers and
streams and then the development of the extensive coalfields around
Wigan supplied the fuel to feed the power hungry machinery. Finally, there was a plentiful supply of labour as families moved from
the hill top sheep farms into the expanding towns and villages to
work the looms and turn the wheels of industry.

In a very short time, smoke and soot filled the air and the once
clear streams and rivers became lifeless valleys of polluted squalor.
There are many illustrations in the region of the harsh working

conditions the labourers had to endure and the dirt and filth that covered much of the area. However, now that much of this has been cleaned up, the rivers running once again fast, clear, and supporting wildlife, the lasting legacy of those days is the splendid Victorian architecture of which every town has at least one example.

Bolton

Synonymous with the Lancashire textile industry, Bolton is also an ancient town that predates its expansion due to cotton by many centuries. First settled during the Bronze Age, by the time of the Civil War, this was a market town supporting the surrounding villages. The town saw one of the bloodiest episodes of the war when James Stanley, Earl of Derby, was brought back here by Cromwell's troops after the Royalists had been defeated. In a savage act of revenge for the massacre his army had brought on the town early in the troubles, Stanley was executed and his severed head and body, in separate caskets, were taken back to the family burial place at Ormskirk. Whilst in captivity in the town, Stanley was kept prisoner at Ye Olde Man and Scythe Inn which, dating from 1251, is still standing in Churchgate today.

Dating back to the 14th century, **Smithills Hall** is an impressive building that is situated on an easily defended hill. Brought by

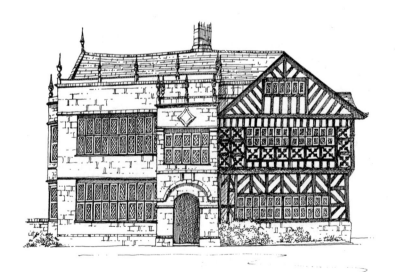

Hall-i'-th'Wood

the Bolton Corporation in the late 1930s, the hall has been beautifully restored and, as well as seeing one of the oldest and best preserved fortified manor houses in the county, visitors can also wander along the hall's wooded nature trail.

Bolton is indeed fortunate as, also on the northern side of the town, is *Hall-i'-th'-Wood*, its second splendid half-timbered house. Dating back to the late 15th century, the house was extended, in stone, in 1591 and again, in 1648, by its then owner, Alexander Norris, a prominent Puritan. A fine example of a wealthy merchant's house, it was saved from dereliction by Lord Leverhulme in 1900 and it has been restored and furnished with displays of fine furniture and interesting items of local importance. However, the hall has a second claim to fame as, for a number of years, Samuel Crompton was one of several tenants here. The inventor, in 1799, of the spinning mule, Crompton's machine was an important factor in the industrialisation of the country's textile industry. Naturally, the hall too has a replica of Crompton's mule on display.

The centre of Bolton is a lasting tribute to the wealth and prosperity generated by the spinning of high quality yarn for which the town was famous. The town hall, opened in 1873, is typical of the classical style of buildings that the Victorian town fathers had built. The hall is still the town's central point and it is now surrounded by the recently refurbished pedestrianised shopping malls, market hall, and the celebrated *Octagon Theatre*. The town's excellent *Museum and Art Gallery* is also well worth a visit as not only are there collections of natural history, geology, and Egyptian antiques here but also some fine 18th and 19th century English water colours and some contemporary British paintings and graphics.

Around Bolton

Horwich   *Map 2 ref F11*
5 miles NW of Bolton on A673
Before the town developed as a centre for the building of steam engines, in the mid-19th century, Horwich was supported by the coal mines and quarries that lay between here and Bolton. In the late 18th century, a local farmer cut some steps down to the Dean Brook, on the town's southeastern boundary, to make the carrying of the coal to the developing textiles mills, by the stream, easier. By the mid-19th century, the company, Gardener and Bazley, had built *Dean Mills* in the valley, along with a purpose-built village, later to

become **Barrow Bridge**, for the mill workers and their families. The workers' village was the inspiration for Benjamin Disraeli's famous novel *Coningsby*.

Just a short distance from the centre of Horwich, **The Green-wood** pub is also close to the magnificent, new Reebok Stadium that is the home of Bolton Wanderers Football Club. Celebrating its centenary in 1999, The Greenwood is a grand, typical late Victo-

The Greenwood

rian building that is hard to miss. Ably run since 1997 by Kath and Chris Ware, this well-decorated pub has retained its high ceilings which make this a light and airy place. As well as the open plan bar area, where an excellent range of well-kept ales are served, there is also a separate restaurant area where a delicious and extensive menu of tasty bar snacks and meals are served at both lunchtime and in the evening. As well as the superb food and drink, Kath and Chris also lay on musical entertainment throughout the week for their customers. All in all, it is not surprising that The Greenwood is a popular pub and, with the Lancashire County Bowling Green to the rear, where visitors with their own bowls can join in a game or two, there is plenty on offer for everyone. *The Greenwood, Chorley New Road, Horwich, Lancashire BL6 6JZ Tel: 01204 468307*

Anderton   *Map 2 ref F11*
6 miles NW of Bolton off A673

Situated in its own extensive grounds at Anderton, just outside Horwich, **The Squirrel Inn** has to be one of the best family pubs in the country. Built in the 1960s, on the site of the previous Squirrel

The Squirrel Inn

Inn, the pub is comfortable and spacious inside with plenty of room for everyone. Both the bar areas and the restaurant are well decorated and furnished and there is also a dedicated children's play room with child-size pool table and slot machines. Open all day, every day, there is something for everyone at the Squirrel. The bar serves a choice of three cask conditioned real ales as well as the more usual brews and lagers and the landlord and lady, Trevor and Gillian Millington, also have a fine selection of malt whiskies for those who prefer a stronger tipple. Food is also taken seriously and, as well as the extensive menu, there is an ever changing specials board to tempt even the most jaded palate.

Though this might all seem enough to make The Squirrel Inn the popular place that it is, there is much more besides. There is live musical entertainment on Friday nights in the winter months and, two Sundays a month, there are quiz evenings. However, what makes The Squirrel special are the grounds that not only contain an attractive beer garden but also a wonderful outdoor children's play area complete with sand pit, Wendy house, climbing frames, and swings. Children will also enjoy the squirrel sanctuary, home to both red and tree squirrels as well as rabbits and guinea pigs. *The Squirrel Inn, Bolton Road, Anderton, Lancashire BL6 7RW Tel: 01204 696194*

Turton Bottoms
Map 3 ref G10
4 miles N of Bolton off B6391
Turton Tower is another fine example of a half-timbered house, similar to those in Bolton. Built around an early 15th century pele tower, constructed as a defence against Scottish raiders, this superb Tudor house was used as a farmhouse in the 18th century and

today it is a wonderful museum. As well as the collections of armour, visitors can view the Tudor and Victorian furniture that is
also on display.

Ramsbottom   *Map 3 ref H10*
6 miles NE of Bolton on A676

At one end of the **East Lancashire Railway**, this picturesque village, overlooking the Irwell Valley, is well worth visiting. However,
one of best views of the village and, in deed, the surrounding area
can be found from **Peel Tower** which dominates the skyline. Built
in 1852 to commemorate the life of the area's most famous son, Sir
Robert Peel, the tower is some 128 feet high. Now restored, the
tower itself is occasionally open to the public.

Rebuilt in the 19th century on the site of an alehouse, **The Royal
Oak Hotel**, in the centre of Ramsbottom, was once owned by John
Grant, MP, who featured in one of the novels of Charles Dickens.
Times have changed since those days but, managed by Alice O'Brien,
The Royal Oak Hotel is still offering excellent hospitality to all who
enter. As well as a fine range of beers and ales behind the bar, a
choice of tasty bar meals and snacks are available each lunchtime.
In the evening the atmosphere of this pleasant and comfortable pub
changes as there is generally some form of entertainment laid on

The Royal Oak Hotel

for customers to enjoy. The weekends are particularly popular as there is live music on both Friday and Saturday nights. *The Royal Oak Hotel, 39 Bridge Street, Ramsbottom, Lancashire BL0 9AD Tel: 01706 682756*

In the Market Place of this traditional Lancashire village, opposite Grant Arms Hotel, is **Ramsbottom Victuallers and the Village Restaurant**. This stone building, the end of a terrace of workers' cottages, which dates from 1829, is, today, home to a first class delicatessen and food shop with a superb restaurant on the first floor. Both are owned and run by Ros Hunter and Chris Johnson whose knowledge and passion for free-range, organic ingredients and fine wines is infectious.

Open for lunch and dinner from Wednesday to Saturday and for lunch only on Sunday, the restaurant has, since it opened in 1985, received national acclaim and it features in The Good Food Guide. The unique style of the Village restaurant, a small menu that is

**Ramsbottom Victuallers
and the Village Restaurant**

served at set times, ensures that the imaginatively prepared and presented dishes reach the customers at the peak of their perfection. Locally reared, well-hung beef features heavily and the tradition of seasonality is strictly adhered to, something that seems to be a thing of the past in many other restaurants and shops. Ros, the chef of the partnership, creates menus that offer customers the very best of modern British cuisine whilst Chris, in the manner of an enthusiastic dinner party host, ensures that dinner here, is an experience to savour. As well as the wine list, guests can also take a trip downstairs to the shop to find the perfect accompaniment to their meal. Due to the unusual style of the restaurant it is essential to book a table.

The shop, recently enlarged, is a foodie Aladdin's cave full of tastes and fine ingredients from Britain and around the world which are supplied by small scale farmers and producers, many of whom are known personally by Chris. The fame of the shop, like the restaurant, has spread far and wide and their customers are happy to travel considerable distances to enjoy the pleasures of the excellent foods and wines found here. The occasional newsletters are not only informative but make enjoyable reading and they highlight the new lines as well as the regular food and wine tastings held on the premises. This superb cosmopolitan establishment is a great find for anyone interested in fine food and wine and is certainly well worth a visit. *Ramsbottom Victuallers and Village Restaurant, 16-18 Market Place, Ramsbottom, Lancashire BL0 9HT Tel: 01706 825070 Fax: 01706 822005*

Just a short distance from the centre of Ramsbottom is **The Fusilier**, a pub whose reputation for fine ale and tasty meals has spread far and wide. Until the 1980s, the pub was known by the rather

The Fusilier

sombre name of The Cemetery, but with the help of some find battle scene prints on the walls and the excellent hospitality of the hosts Rita and Ian Coughlin, and their son Nigel and daughter Gillian, this is now a lively and pleasant place to visit. Well decorated and furnished, there is a small restaurant area, for which booking is essential on Sundays, where the delicious menu of traditional and more exciting dishes are served during the day. The bar too offers a varied range of well kept ales and the pub is a member of the Whitbread Cask Ale Club. At the weekend there is Kareoke (Saturday evening) and a quiz night (Sunday) to further add to customers' enjoyment. *The Fusilier, 176 Bolton Road West, Ramsbottom, Lancashire BL0 9PE Tel: 01706 822485*

Holcombe
Map 3 ref H10

5 miles NE of Bolton off A56

Holcombe village, just to the south of Ramsbottom, is one of the oldest surviving communities around Ramsbottom itself, dating back to the 14th century. ***The Andertons Restaurant***, owned and personally run by Pam Hazel with her daughter, Emma, who is an experienced chef, is situated on the lower slopes of Holcombe Hill. The building, which survived a Zeppelin bomb attack in 1916, has been converted from an old post office, which in turn was converted from three cottages. The tower on the hill behind the restaurant was erected in memory of Sir Robert Peel the founder of the modern police force.

The restaurant, which is open in the evening from Wednesday to Sunday, and for lunch from Friday to Sunday, has a cosy, olde worlde

The Andertons Restaurant

appearance with a delicious choice of menus to match. A combination of traditional English cuisine with several continental alternatives, the light lunchtime selection is complemented by a tantalising à la carte evening menu. Licensed for diners, The Andertons Restaurant also welcomes children and such is its popularity that booking is essential at weekends. *The Andertons Restaurant, 18-20 Holcombe Village, Ramsbottom, Lancashire BL8 4NZ Tel: 01706 825702*

Bury   Map 3 ref H11
6 miles E of Bolton on A58

Looking at Bury today it seems hard to imagine that, at one time, this typical Lancashire mill town had a castle. A settlement probably existed here in the Bronze Age and there is certainly evidence that the Romans passed through this area. By the 12th century, the town was the manor of the Norman de Bury family and, in the mid-14th century, the land came under the ownership of the Pilkingtons. Though the age of the castle is not known, its site is now covered by a 19th-century drill hall, it was dismantled following the Battle of Bosworth in 1485 where Henry VII defeated Richard III. Unlucky Thomas Pilkington had backed the wrong side.

It is certainly people rather than buildings for which the town is famous. Apart from the hapless Thomas Pilkington, whose family, centuries later, made a fortune in glass at St Helens, both the Peel family and John Kay helped to shape the town's future. John Kay was, of course, the inventor of the flying shuttle, which although transforming the life of the weaver, did nothing towards creating personal wealth for Kay. With no head for business, Kay moved to France, died penniless, and lies buried in an unmarked grave.

Before Robert Peel Senior opened his Ground Calico Printing Works in 1770, this small market town lay amid green and fertile land. However, the opening of the works along with the subsequent mills, print and bleach works so dominated this part of the Irwell Valley that not only did they transform the landscape but also heavily polluted the river. At the height of the valley's production it was said that anyone falling into the river would dissolve before they had a chance to drown. Today, thankfully, the valley towns are once again clean and the river clear and fast flowing.

With the family fortune gleaned from these prosperous mills, Robert Peel, born in the town in 1788, was able to fund his illustrious career in politics. Famous for the repeal of the Corn Laws, Robert Peel was also at the forefront of the setting up of the modern police force - hence their nickname 'Bobbies'. In the Bury's market square is a bronze statue to the town's most famous son.

Bury's **Art Gallery and Museum**, home to the renowned Thomas Wrighley collection of Victorian oil paintings and water colours, also hosts a lively programme of temporary exhibitions and the museum features a cobbled street of reconstructed shops and dwellings from Bury's past. The history of Lancashire's famous regiment, from its foundation in 1688, is displayed in the **Lancashire Fusiliers Museum**.

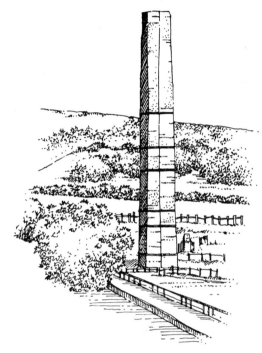

Burrs Country Park

On the outskirts of the town lies **Burrs Country Park** which, as well as offering a wide range of activities, also has an interesting industrial trail around this historic mill site.

Walmersley
Map 3 ref H11
2 miles NE of Bolton on A56

Hidden away in the village of Walmersley, just north of Bury, is **Hark to Dandler**, an attractive pub dating from the mid-19th century that is thought to have originally been a vicarage. During a recent refurbishment a very old child's coffin was found, full of early 19th-century artefacts, behind the cellar walls and, along with the two resident ghosts, this certainly adds an air of mystery to the pub. The name though is more easily explained as it is named after a lead dog of the local hunt. The licensees, Elaine and Jim, only came here in January 1998 but they have not only taken the pub's unusual finds in their stride but have also used their years of expe-

Hark to Dandler

rience to provide a warm and welcoming atmosphere to all their customers. Open every day, all day Friday to Sunday, an excellent range of JW Lee beers and ales are served behind the bar, as well as the usual ales and lagers, and, at lunchtime, tasty bar snacks are available. This is also a lively pub with not only a regular quiz held each Thursday evening but also darts, dominoes, and cribbage games on the go as well as sponsorship of a ladies rounders team. *Hark to Dandler, 156 Old Road, Walmersley, Bury, Lancashire BL9 6SA Tel: 0161 764 2116*

Tottington

Map 3 ref G11

4 miles N of Bolton on B6213

An unspoilt farming town on the edge of moorland, Tottington escaped the industrialisation of many of its neighbours due to its, then, isolated position and it is still an attractive place to visit.

The **Hark to Towler**, in the centre of the town, is very much a locals pub that happily welcomes visitors. Dating back to the 1800s, this imposing red brick pub's unusual name means call - hark - to the lead dog of the hunt - towler. Since they came here in 1994, Bob and Lesley Birtwistle, the landlord and lady, have made this a very popular place indeed. As well as the extensive range of bitters, ales, lagers, and ciders served here, Hark to Towler is the place to come to for live music. Well known and popular groups, from across many

Hark to Towler

fields of music, play here each Saturday night and on alternate Friday evenings. Certainly, the place for those who enjoy a good drink and a lively atmosphere, there is also a Kareoke and disco every other Thursday evening to which all are welcome. *Hark to Towler, 43 Market Street, Tottington, near Bury, Lancashire BL8 4AA Tel: 01204 883856*

In the small village of **Walshaw**, just south of Tottington, can be found **The Victoria Hotel**, which was originally built in 1815 as a row of weavers' cottages but, in 1860, it became a licensed premises

The Victoria Hotel

run by Titus Turner and his family. Still a family run hotel today, this attractive hotel is open all day, every day, and offers customers a fine selection of well-kept real ales, such as Boddingtons, Theakstons, and Flowers, as well as all the usual beers, lagers, and ciders. The surroundings are cosy and leading off from the main bar area are several small rooms which offer comfort and intimacy. The comprehensive menu of delicious, home-cooked meals is served each evening and at lunchtime from Friday to Sunday. Popular and well frequented by locals, this is certainly a place worth finding. However, this is not all that the Victoria Hotel has to offer the visitor as there are also six superb en-suite guest rooms that are as comfortable and charming as the rest of the hotel. Those touring the area will be interested to learn that The Chetham Arms at Chapeltown is run by the same family and it too offers the same excellent hospitality to all. *The Victoria Hotel, 12 Hall Street, Walshaw, near Bury, Lancashire BL8 3BD Tel: 0161 761 5801*

Rochdale

Lying in a shallow valley formed by the little River Roch, the town is surrounded, to the north and east, by the slopes of the Pennines that are often snow covered in winter. With its origins in medieval times, the town, like so many others in Lancashire, expanded with the booming cotton industry and, once prosperous, its Town Hall rivals that of Manchester in style if not in size.

However, it is not textiles for which Rochdale is famous but as its role as the birthplace of the Co-operative Movement. In carefully restored Toad Lane, to the north of the town centre, is the world's first Co-op shop, the *Rochdale Pioneers*. The Co-op movement now represents a staggering 700 million members in 90 countries around the world and the celebration of its 150th anniversary in 1994 focused attention on Rochdale and the *Pioneers' Co-operative Museum*.

The town has some other famous sons and daughters and these include the famous 19th century political thinker, John Bright, the celebrated singer Gracie Fields, and Cyril Smith, its long-standing former Liberal Member of Parliament.

The beginning of the 19th century also saw the birth of the Rochdale Canal, a brave piece of civil engineering that traversed the Pennines to link the River Mersey with the Calder and Hebble Navigation. Some 33 miles in length and with 92 locks, it must be one of toughest canals ever built and, though the towpath can still

Pioneers' Co-operative Museum

be walked, the last commercial boat passed through the locks in 1937. Officially abandoned in 1952, some sections of the canal have been restored.

Between Rochdale and Littleborough lies Hollingworth Lake, originally built as a supply reservoir for the canal, but for many years a popular area for recreation known colloquially as 'the Weavers' Seaport', as cotton workers unable to enjoy a trip to the seaside came here. Now part of the *Hollingworth Lake Country Park* and with a fine visitor centre, there are a number of pleasant walks around its shores.

Dating back to the 1870s, *The Golden Ball* lies in a quiet part of Rochdale yet it is only a few minutes walk to the town centre and the local football ground. This imposing red brick pub, named after a sailing ship, is typical of the architecture of the time and the original stained glass in the front windows is one of the several features that has stood the test of time. A popular pub with locals, this is landlord Philip Smith's first venture in the licensing trade and, though new to the business, he has certainly made his mark. As well as the excellent range of ales, beers, and lagers served at the bar, there is also a tasty list of bar meals served until the early evening. With a warm and friendly atmosphere, and very busy at weekends, there is also plenty going on here. As well as the usual pool and darts, there are several football teams run from the pub

The Golden Ball

and, for those who enjoy music, there is a disco on Friday evenings and Kareoke on Saturdays. *The Golden Ball, 225 Spotland Road, Rochdale, Lancashire OL12 7AG Tel: 01706 646694*

North of Rochdale

Edenfield   *Map 3 ref H10*
7 miles NW of Rochdale on A680
The village lies on the banks of the River Irwell, as its drops from the moorland of the Forest of Rossendale and into its valley in which lie the many mill towns and villages of Lancashire.

Housed within the Horse and Jockey public house, in the centre of the village, is ***Edenfield Chinese Restaurant***, a true flavour of the orient in the heart of northwest England. Elegant and stylish, the restaurant is designed to transport customers from Lancashire to the Cantonese region of China even before they get a taste of the delicious dishes to come. Well known and highly regarded for the excellence of the cuisine, particularly the range of Chinese vegetarian dishes, the restaurant has an enviable reputation of which the Chinese chefs are justly proud. The menu, which features many favourite dishes, is extensive and varied and will provide the more adventurous guest with a bewildering choice. Open each evening, except non-Bank Holiday Mondays, it is always a good idea to book as this is a popular place in the area. Edenfield Chinese Restaurant

Edenfield Chinese Restaurant

also offers a take away service. *Edenfield Chinese Restaurant, 85 Market Street, Edenfield, Lancashire BL0 0JQ Tel: 01706 821688*

Whitworth   Map 3 ref I10
3 miles N of Rochdale on A671

This pleasant town, of cottages and farms, lies on Pennine moorland above Rochdale. Between here and Bacup, a distance of only seven miles, the railway line, another feat of Victorian engineering, climbs over 500 feet. Not surprisingly, there were various problems during its construction, such as frequent landslides, but once constructed this was a picturesque line with attractive station houses with neat well tendered gardens along the route. The line, like so many, fell to the extensive railway cuts of the 1960s.

The Dog and Partridge, in the centre of the town, is an impressive and easy to spot white-painted listed building situated on a corner. Dating back to the 19th century, trams used to run right outside the pub but, today, most visitors arrive on foot or by car (there is parking to the rear). Since arriving here at the end of 1997, landlord and lady, Michael and Anne Neil, have breathed fresh air into the inn and established it as one of the more popular places in the surrounding area. From the bar a full range of ales, including Samsons Smooth and Marstons Pedigree, are available along with all the usual beers, lagers, and ciders. At lunchtime, and again

The Dog and Partridge

in the evening, a varied menu of speciality cuisine dishes, such as Chinese and Indian, are served in the separate, comfortable dining area. This pleasant pub, with its friendly atmosphere and tasteful decor, is an ideal place for a good pint and a delicious, different pub meal. *The Dog and Partridge, 264 Market Street, Whitworth, Lancashire OL12 8PW Tel: 01706 715629*

Healey   Map 3 ref I10
1 mile N of Rochdale on A671

Lying in the valley of the River Spodden, this old village, now almost engulfed by the outer reaches of Rochdale, is an area rich in wildlife as well as folklore. Nearby is Robin Hood's Well, one of a number of springs feeding the river. Here, it is said, sometime in the 12th century the Earl of Huntington was lured to the well by a witch pretending to be his nursemaid. Once at the well, the witch told the young man that he would never inherit his earldom unless he had her magic ring as a means of identification. Gazing into the well, Robin got such a fright that he fainted and the witch took off on her broomstick. Emerging from the well the King of the Fairies, gave the lad his own ring and told him to go up into Healey Dell and interrupt the witches whilst they were hatching their next spell. Doing as he was instructed Robin entered the coven and threw the ring into their cauldron where upon there was a great flash of light and the witches were reduced to evil looking fairies destined to live forever in the Fairy chapel.

Opened in 1972, **Healey Dell Nature Reserve** does not promise visitors sightings of either witches or fairies but there is a wealth of wildlife to be discovered along the nature trails. This is an ancient area which has only been interrupted by the construction of the commercially nonviable Rochdale to Bacup railway in the late 19th century. The oak and birch woodland on the northern river bank is all that remains of a prehistoric forest and, whilst the owners of Healey Hall made some impact, little has changed here for centuries.

Littleborough   *Map 3 ref I10*
3 miles NE of Rochdale on A58

Unfortunately little more than a suburb of Rochdale today, this small town lies on the main route between Lancashire and Yorkshire first laid down by the Romans. The road takes in **Blackstone Edge** and here are some of the best preserved parts of the Roman structure. At the summit is a medieval cross, the **Aigin Stone**, which offers spectacular views over Lancashire right to the coast.

South of Rochdale

Shaw   *Map 3 ref J11*
3 miles SE of Rochdale on A633

A typical mill town, founded on the wealth of the cotton trade, this was also a market town for the surrounding area. Closed since 1932, **Jubilee Colliery**, to the northeast of the town centre, has been reclaimed as a nature reserve and it is now an attractive haven for wildlife in the Beal Valley.

The Kings Arms, in the centre of Shaw, was built in the 1960s but for much of its life it has been called The Big Lamp, a name still

The Kings Arms

used today, as a large street lamp used to stand opposite the pub. Very much a place for locals to meet and catch up on the news and gossip, manager Julie King has created a warm and friendly atmosphere that certainly makes this a pleasant place for a drink: a range of beers and ales are available from the bar as well as the usual lagers and ciders. Once a month, The Kings Arms hosts live entertainment shows on a Friday evening and as well as the regular Saturday night pool competition there is plenty happening throughout the week to add to customers enjoyment of the pub. *The Kings Arms, 3 Oldham Road, Shaw, Lancashire OL2 8RZ Tel: 01706 841202*

Delph   Map 3 ref J11
7 miles SE of Rochdale on A6052

Taking its name from the old English for quarry, this is probably a reference to the bakestone quarries found to the north of the village. Also close by, and high on a hill above the village, lies **Castleshaw**, one of a series of forts the Romans built on their military road between Chester and York. The banks and ditches give visitors an excellent indication of the scale of the fort and many of the items found during recent excavations are on show in the Saddleworth Museum.

The White Lion pub dates back to 1760 when it was originally built as farm cottages adjacent to a farm. As a result of its beginnings, the interior of this traditional inn is particularly charming with plenty of nooks and crannies as well as intimate small rooms.

The White Lion

The displays of interesting artefacts and memorabilia add to the atmosphere and age of the premises and one room, in particular, will interest sports fans as it is dedicated to the cricketer, Sunny Ramadin, who once ran the pub. Today, this freehouse is owned and run by Barbara and Harry Whitehead who, with plenty of experience in the trade, have turned The White Lion into one of the most popular pubs in the area. As well as a fine choice of real ales, the pub has gained a reputation for the extensive menu of delicious meals that are served at lunchtime Friday to Sunday and Bank Holiday Mondays and early evening from Monday to Friday. A super pub, with charming hosts, that is the ideal place for a good meal and a well-kept pint of beer. *The White Lion, 1 Delph Lane, Delph, Lancashire OL3 5HX Tel: 01457 874435*

Dobcross
Map 3 ref J11

7 miles S of Rochdale off A6052

This attractive Pennine village, once the commercial heart of the district of Saddleworth, retains many of its original weavers' cottages, clothiers, and merchants' houses, and little has changed around the village square in the last 200 years. Used as the location for the film, *Yanks*, Dobcross is also famous as the birthplace of the giant Platt Brothers Textile Machinery business which was, in the latter part of the 19th century, the largest such machine manufacturing firm in the world.

Uppermill
Map 3 ref J11

8 miles S of Rochdale on A62

Of the villages that make up Saddleworth, Uppermill is the most central. It is certainly home to the area's oldest building, **Saddleworth Parish Church** which was originally built in the 12th century by the Stapletons as their family chapel. Extended over the years, there are several interesting features including a gravestone to commemorate the Bill-o-Jacks murders. In 1832, the people of Saddleworth were stunned to learn that the landlord of the Moorcock Inn and his son had been bludgeoned to death. Several thousand people turned out for the funeral but the case was never solved.

Housed in an old mill building on the banks of the Huddersfield Canal, the **Saddleworth Museum**, tells the story of this once isolated area and there is a reconstruction of an 18th century weaver's cottage as well as a collection of woollen textile machinery, local history gallery, and local art exhibitions.

Also here is the **Brownhill Visitor Centre**, which not only has information on the northern section of the Tame Valley but also exhibitions on local wildlife and the area's history.

Diggle *Map 3 ref J11*

8 miles S of Rochdale off A62

Above the village, on **Diggle Moor** lies Brun Clough Farm where, it is said, the cries of child slaves who were ill treated in the early days of the textile mills can still be heard coming from the outhouses. Part of the **Oldham Way** footpath, a 30 mile scenic walk through the countryside on the edge of the Peak District National Park, crosses the moorland.

Much of the village itself is a conservation area, where the pre-industrial weaving community has been preserved along with some of the traditional skills. However, Diggle Mill, which used to operate the second largest waterwheel in the country, no longer exists.

The Huddersfield Narrow Canal, completed in 1811, is one of the three canals that crossed the difficult terrain of the Pennines and joined Lancashire with Yorkshire. The entrance to the **Standedge Canal Tunnel**, the longest and highest canal tunnel in Britain, lies in the village. The last cargo boat passed through the tunnel in 1921 and following a long period of closure, it has now been re-opened.

Situated on high ground overlooking the village and its valley, **New Barn** is the delightful home of Dorothy and Alan Rhodes. This

New Barn

is a working sheep farm but guests to this wonderful bed and breakfast establishment will see little evidence of the running of the farm. As the name might suggest, New Barn was originally one of the outbuildings and, in the mid-1960s, it was completely refurbished to created this attractive and comfortable home. Guests have a choice of four charming rooms, all with panoramic views over Saddleworth Moor, and there is also a residents' lounge that is ideal for relaxing. Everyone is treated to a delicious home-cooked breakfast and, though there are no evening meals served, packed lunches are available. Both children and pets (by arrangement) are welcome and private fishing is also available in a private pond that has been well stocked with brown trout. *New Barn, Harrop Green Farm, Diggle, Saddleworth, Lancashire OL3 5LW Tel: 01457 873937 Mobile: 0467 308985*

Denshaw   *Map 3 ref J11*
5 miles S of Rochdale on A640

In the moorland above the village is the source of the River Tame, which flows through the Saddleworth area and eventually joins the River Goyt at Stockport. A charming 18th century village, its Scandinavian name would suggest that there has been a settlement here for many centuries.

Found just outside the village of Denshaw, one of the six which makes up Saddleworth, **Moorlands Caravan Park** is, as its name suggests, a park surrounded by miles of open moorland. However, the site is also convenient for the trans-Pennine motorway (the M62) and the towns of both Lancashire and Yorkshire. Though the site is surrounded by spectacular and, in bad weather, very bleak moorland, the caravans are intermingled with trees and shrubbery which is not only attractive but also provides privacy.

Moorlands Caravan Park

There has been a caravan and camping site here since World War II and Moorlands has been in the same family since 1986 with Susan and Stephen Ashurst being the present owners and mangers. Essentially a residential site, there are facilities for 20 touring caravans on either hard or soft standing as well as several caravans available for hire for a quiet and peaceful self-catering holiday. Both children and well behaved pets are welcome, though there are not special amenities for children, and the site also has an up to the minute shower block, washrooms, and a laundry. For those who enjoy spectacular scenery and an out of the way location, Moorlands Caravan Park has a lot to offer. *Moorlands Caravan Park, Rough Hey, Ripponden Road, Denshaw, Saddleworth, Lancashire OL3 5UN Tel: 01457 874348*

Newhey   *Map 3 ref I11*
3 miles S of Rochdale on A640

Just to the north lies the **Piethorne Valley**, with its five reservoirs that are surrounded by excellent moorland walking country. As well as the excellent trail leaflets, there are guided walks and events organized in the valley.

Milnrow   *Map 3 ref I11*
2 miles S of Rochdale on A640

It was to this small industrial town, in the foothills of the Pennines, that John Collier came as the schoolmaster in 1729. Then a woollen handloom weaving village, Collier is perhaps better known as Tim Bobbin, the first of the Lancashire dialect poets. Collier remained in Milnrow for the rest of his life and, drinking rather more than he should, he earned extra money by selling his verse and painting pub signs.

Dating back to the early 1800s, the **Tim Bobbin**, named after a local schoolmaster, is an attractive and welcoming pub managed by Mark and Nicky. Beautifully decorated and furnished throughout, there are quarry tiled floors, leaded windows, heavily beamed ceilings, and an open fire, which all go to make this a pleasing and relaxing place for a drink. From the bar customers can enjoy a range of bitters, ales, ciders, and lagers and there are also a range of tasty bar snacks and meals available at lunchtime. In the evenings, at the weekend, the Tim Bobbin livens up with either a disco or Kareoke on Saturday nights and, on Sunday evening, a quiz. All are welcome and are sure to enjoy the friendly atmosphere of this well run pub. *Tim Bobbin, 3 Dale Street, Milnrow, Lancashire OL16 3LH Tel: 01706 658992*

The Tim Bobbin

CHAPTER SEVEN
Isle of Man

Peel Castle

Chapter 7 - Area Covered

*For precise location of places please refer to the colour
maps found at the rear of the book.*

7
The Isle of Man

Introduction

This island is perhaps best known for its annual TT motorcycle races, its tailless cat, Manx kippers, and as a tax haven for the wealthy. However, there is much more to this beautiful island which, set in the heart of the Irish Sea, is truly a world apart. With around 100 miles of coastline and several resorts, each with its own individual style and character, although the Isle of Man is by no means large, there is plenty to interest the visitor.

This magical place became an island around 10,000 years ago when the melt water of the Ice Age raised the sea level. Soon afterwards, the first settlers arrived, working and developing the island into the landscape seen today. The distinctive influences of the various cultures who have lived here still remain, leaving a land with a unique and colourful heritage.

Among the first arrivals were the Vikings and evidence of their era, from the early chieftains to the last Norse King, abounds throughout the Isle of Man. Against the skyline on the seaward side of road between Ballaugh and Bride are some ancient hilltop Viking burial mounds and, at the ancient castle in Peel, an archaeological dig revealed many hidden Viking treasures which are now on display at the Manx Museum in Douglas.

Despite their reputation for plunder, rape, and pillage, the Vikings also made some positive contributions to life on the island, not least of which was the establishment of the Manx governmental system, known as Tynwald. The Manx name for Tynwald Hill is 'Cronk Keeill Eoin', the hill of St John's Church. Although there is no evidence to confirm the story that it contains earth from all of the 17 parish churches here, it is not unlikely that token portions of soil were added to the mound in accordance with Norse tradition.

The Tynwald ceremony continues today with an annual meeting of the island's governors on Midsummer's Day at the ancient parliament field at St John's, where Manx citizens can also petition parliament. This makes the Isle of Man an independent country, with its own taxes, currency (British currency is also acceptable), and native language - fortunately everyone speaks English.

The island's famous three-legged symbol seems to have been adopted in the 13th century as the amorial bearings of the native Kings of the Isle of Man, whose dominion also included the Hebrides. After 1266, when the native dynasty ended and control of the island passed, briefly, to the Crown of Scotland and then permanently to the Crown of England, the emblem was retained, and among the earliest surviving representations are those on the Manx Sword of State, though to have been made in 1300. The Three Legs also appeared on Manx coinage from the 17th to the 19th century, and are still seen in everyday use in the form of the official Manx flag.

Why the Three Legs were adopted as the Royal Arms of the Manx Kingdom is unknown. Many heraldic emblems have no meaning and are simply chosen because they are distinctive. This may be the case with the Three Legs, though the emblem as such - something between a cross and a swastika - has a long history reaching far back into pagan times and was originally a symbol of the sun, the seat of power and light.

Douglas

The island's capital, Douglas is also a lively resort with its two mile long promenade, the focus of the island's nightlife. From dawn to dusk, visitors can take a leisurely ride along this wonderful promenade aboard the ***Douglas Bay Horse Tramway***, a remarkable and beautiful reminder of a bygone era. It was the brainchild of a civil engineer, Thomas Lightfoot, who retired to the island and, seeing the need for a public transport system along this elegant promenade, designed the system still in use today. That the Douglas Tramway has survived until the 1990s is remarkable especially as, at the beginning of this century, attempts were made to electrify the line and extend the Manx electric railway along the promenade.

There is a story often told about the horses that pull the trams, which concerns a parrot that lived in a cage at a hotel close to one of the tram's stops. The bird learnt to mimic the sound of the tram's starting bell and used to practise this skill constantly. The tram horses would stop when the they heard the bell and start off again immediately before the passengers could alight as the bird joined in the fun.

Another delightful means of travel is the Victorian **Steam Railway** that runs between Douglas and Port Erin. Following the line of the cliff tops, the memorable journey also travels through blue-bell woods and through steep-sided rocky cuttings. This section of line is all that remains of a railway that once served the whole of the island.

The Manx cat, that has no tail, is probably the most famous export from the Isle of Man. There are several stories of how the cat lost its tail but one, in particular, is delightful. At the time that Noah was building the Ark there were two Manx cats, complete

Horse Tram, Douglas

with tails. Noah sent for all the animals to come to the Ark, two by two, but the Manx cats replied that there was plenty of time and continued to play outside. Finally, when the cats did decided to board the Ark, Noah was just slamming the door and the cats lost their tails. A variation on this tale, is that one of the cats reached the Ark safely, the other had its tail chopped off by the closing doors. The tailless cat went on to become the Manx cat and the one who managed to keep its tail became the ever grinning Cheshire cat. In the heart of Douglas can be found the **Manx Cattery**, where tales and no tails are revealed!

No trip to the island is complete without a visit to the **Manx Museum**, where the Story of Man film gives a dramatic and vivid portrayal of the island's unique history. The exciting gallery presentations include the superb National Art Gallery as well as taking in many other aspects of life on the island including the famous TT races.

One of the Isle of Man's most famous landmarks, the **Tower of Refuge**, looks out over Douglas Bay. Sir William Hilary, founder of the Royal National Lifeboat Institution, lived in a mansion overlooking the bay and, following a near disaster in 1830 when the Royal Mail Steam Packet *St George* was driven on to rocks in high seas, Hilary launched the Douglas lifeboat. Miraculously, all the crew of the St George were saved without the loss of one lifeboat man, despite the extremely treacherous conditions. It was following this incident that Hilary decided that a form of refuge should be built for shipwrecked mariners to shelter in and so, with Hilary laying the foundation stone in 1832, the Tower of Refuge was built on Conister Rock out in the bay.

Finally, perched on a headland overlooking Douglas Bay is a camera obscura known as the **Great Union Camera**. The camera was originally situated on the old iron pier, but when this was demolished in the 1870s the camera was resited on Douglas Head. In the camera, the natural daylight in focused on to a white panel through a simple system of lenses and angled mirrors and so provides a living image of the scene outside. At first apparently still, as with a photograph, viewers soon become fascinated as the 'picture' begins to move.

Standing on Harris Promenade and overlooking Douglas Bay is the impressive **Sefton Hotel**, one of the best hotel's on the island that is also very much a part of island life. As well as offering first class accommodation in a choice of superb en-suite rooms, many of which have a sea view and a balcony, the hotel offers guests and

The Sefton Hotel

nonresidents an excellent range of facilities. The Dining Room, a popular dining venue with island inhabitants, is open for breakfast and à la carte dinner and provides the perfect dining experience. Elegantly decorated and furnished in a style reminiscent of the days of the Raj, the evening à la carte menu is complemented by an extensive wine list.

For informal eating morning coffee and afternoon tea the first floor Harris's Morning Room is ideal. Customers can sit on deep comfortable sofas, taking in the fine views over Douglas Bay, and enjoy a delicious range of light lunches and snacks in what is an excellent and imaginative coffee shop. The Tramshunters Arms, adjacent to the main hotel, is highly recommended by CAMRA and is the island's leading real ale pub. Traditionally decorated and furnished, not only is there a fine selection of real ales served here on tap but the pub also has its own bistro-style menu of original dishes.

Residents of the hotel can also enjoy membership of the hotel's Fountain Health and Leisure Club which provides all the usual health facilities in luxurious surroundings which certainly make exercising a relaxing experience. Finally, the Sefton Hotel has a recently created atrium garden, the ideal place for a quiet moment or a game of chess that, along with the other superb facilities will take the hotel and its guests well into the 21st century. *Sefton Hotel, Harris Promenade, Douglas, Isle of Man IM1 2RW Tel: 01624 626011 Fax: 01624 676004*

The Ainsdale Hotel is a small, family run establishment which lies just off the Central Promenade and is within a short walk of the town centre and the casino. This large late Victorian house, situated in a quiet terrace, has an attractive patio area at the front which is furnished with plenty of comfortable seating as it makes the ideal sun trap and is also home to a vibrant display of colourful window boxes and tubs of flowers. Inside, the hotel is charming and everything is done to ensure that, whilst here, guests have an enjoyable, relaxing stay and are made to feel at home. There are 13 guest rooms, most of which have en-suite bathrooms, as well as a cosy residents' lounge and bright and airy dining room. A hearty, home-cooked breakfast is served each morning and both evening meals

The Ainsdale Hotel

and light suppers can be provided by prior arrangement. *The Ainsdale Hotel, 2 Empire Terrace, off Central Promenade, Douglas, Isle of Man IM1 4LE Tel & Fax: 01624 676695*

Just a stone's throw from the Promenade and beach, **The Dragon's Nest** is a charming guest house that offers its guests the very best in holiday accommodation. The house dates from the 1890s and, when Aly and Kev moved here in the summer of 1997, they completely refurbished the house to create this luxurious home. Kev is an astrologer and, along with the Celtic links on the island, they renamed and have given each of the 10 comfortable guest bedrooms

The Dragon's Nest

the name of a dragon. The excellent and stylish decor of the guest rooms is mirrored in the cosy residents' lounge and in the dining room where a delicious breakfast is served each morning and, by prior arrangement, evening meals. Although Aly and Kev are relative newcomers to the Isle of Man, they have already found numerous interesting places to visit and happily pass on the information to their guests who also have free entry into the snooker club adjacent to The Dragon's Nest. *The Dragon's Nest, 7 Castle Mona Avenue, Douglas, Isle of Man IM2 4EA Tel: 01624 623360*

Situated on Loch Promenade, overlooking Douglas Bay, **Admiral House Hotel** is certainly one of the island's finest establishments as well as one of the Isle of Man's landmarks. Built during the Victorian age, when it was known as the Regent, during World War II the hotel was commandeered by the Admiralty as a home for Chief Petty Officers as they trained the new recruits before they went into action. After the war, the building was decommissioned and returned to the more sedate life of a hotel. During the 1980s, it was redeveloped as the luxury establishment it is today and, in memory of the important role it played some 40 years before, the hotel was renamed Admiral House. The hotel is now owned and personally run by Ginny and Mike Proffitt. Mike is a local man who, after purchasing the hotel, learnt that his father, Joe, was one of the Petty Officers stationed here during war and this was where he met Mike's mother, Edith.

Today, the Admiral House Hotel offers guests the very best in accommodation and cuisine. As well as the 30 magnificent en-suite rooms available, the hotel's first floor Boncompte's restaurant is not

The Admiral House Hotel

only exclusive but one of the north of England's finest eating establishments. Open to both residents and nonresidents, booking is always essential and well worth while. The menu, complemented by a fine wine list, is a delicious array of delightfully prepared dishes that make the most the freshest ingredients, including a range of fish. For less formal eating, La Tasca, situated on the ground floor, is an authentic Spanish restaurant and tapas bar that also has an Spanish chef. *Admiral House Hotel, 12 Loch Promenade, Douglas, Isle of Man IM1 2LX Tel: 01624 629551 Fax: 01624 675021*

Situated in the centre of the promenade, in a row of charming Georgian terrace houses, is **Bentlea Guest House**, a delightful place with a relaxed and pleasant atmosphere. As might be expected from its superb position, there are fantastic sea views from all the front facing rooms, including several of the five en-suite guest rooms. As well as offering all guests a comfortable and restful night's sleep, the Bentlea has much more besides. Delicious home-cooked breakfasts are served in the dining room, which still retains its original stained glass window, and there are a selection of board games in

Bentlea Guest House

the comfortable lounge. To the front of the house, the small terrace garden not only contains comfortable seating where guests can make the most the sunshine, but the mass of flower-filled tubs, pots, and hanging baskets make a magnificent, colourful display. All in all the Bentlea is an excellent home-from-home where visitors are warmly received and well looked after. *Bentlea Guest House, 8 The Esplanade, Douglas, Isle of Man, IM2 4LR Tel: 01624 673879*

North of Douglas

Port Groudle   Map 5 ref O5
3 miles N of Douglas on A11

Close to Port Groudle lies **Groundle Glen**, a deep and in places rocky valley with a bubbling stream running through its length. Excellent specimens of beech grow in the upper sections of the glen whilst, lower down, pines and larches are abundant. There is also a small waterwheel in the lower half of the glen. Railway enthusiasts will be delighted to learn that a miniature railway operates, on certain days, in the glen.

Laxey   Map 5 ref O4
5 miles N of Douglas on A2

Set in a deep, wooded valley, this village is one of interesting contrasts. Tracing the river up from its mouth at the small tidal harbour leads the walker into **Laxey Glen**, one of the island's 17 National

Glens that are preserved and maintained by the Forestry department of the government

Further up the glen is one of the island's most famous sights, the **Great Laxey Wheel** that marks the site of a once thriving mining community. Known as the **Lady Isabella Wheel**, with a circumference of 228 feet, a diameter of 72 feet, and a top platform some 72 feet off the ground, it is the largest waterwheel in the world.

It was Robert Casement, an engineer at the mines, who constructed this mechanical wonder and designed it to pump 250 gallons of water a minute from a depth of 200 fathoms. Officially opened in 1854, it was named the Lady Isabella after the wife of the then Lieutenant Governor of the Isle of Man. After considerable repair and reconstruction work, the wheel now oper-

Great Laxey Wheel

ates just as it did when it first opened and it stands as a monument to Victorian engineering as well as the island's industrial heritage.

Situated above Laxey, in a beautiful natural glen, are the magnificent **Ballalheanagh Gardens**. The valley, of steep sides with winding paths and a crystal clear stream running through the bottom, is packed with rhododendrons, shrubs, bulbs, and ferns and is certainly a gardeners' paradise well worth seeking out.

From Laxey station, the **Snaefell Mountain Railway** carries visitors to the top of the island's only mountain. Built in 1895, the six original tram cars still climb the steep gradients to **Snaefell**'s 2,036 foot summit and this is certainly the way to travel for those unwilling to walk. Those reaching the top are rewarded with outstanding views of the whole island and out over the sea to Ireland, Scotland, and England. There is also a café on the summit offering welcome refreshments.

Ramsey   *Map 5 ref P3*
12 miles N of Douglas on A18

This northernmost resort on the island is an attractive coastal town with a cosy harbour that is highly regarded by visiting yachtsmen. Just to the north of the town, lies the **Grove Rural Life Museum**, housed in a pleasantly proportioned Victorian house. Built as the

Ramsey Harbour

summer retreat of Duncan Gibb, a wealthy Victorian shipping merchant from Liverpool, and his family, the rooms within the house have all been restored to their Victorian splendour and stepping into the museum is just like taking a step back in time. The outbuildings have not been neglected and they contain an interesting collection of vehicles and agricultural instruments that were seen on Manx farms in the late 19th century.

Found close to the Grove Museum is **The Hollies**, an attractive, large, modern bungalow that is the home of Julie and Tony Mansfield. Since 1997, this charming couple have been offering outstanding bed and breakfast accommodation in their luxurious en-suite guest room that really would put many hotel rooms to shame. Everything that a guest could wish for has been thoughtfully provided

The Hollies

and, as the only holidaymakers staying here, guests receive personal attention and are made very much to feel one of the family, this includes the adoring attention of Julie and Tony's three friendly dogs, Sacha, Leo, and Chico. To the rear of the bungalow is a lovely garden and patio area that is ideal for sitting in and relaxing after a hard day out exploring the island or just lazing away a summer's afternoon. The garden also overlooks a neighbouring field, owned by the Grove Museum, that is home to a herd of the famous and rare Manx Loaghtan sheep. The Hollies takes guests from April until the end of September. *The Hollies, Richmond Road, Ramsey, Isle of Man, IM8 3PB Tel: 01624 815360*

Point of Ayre   Map 5 ref P1
18 miles N of Douglas on A16

This is the northernmost tip of the island and, not surprisingly, there is a lighthouse situated here. The area around the point is known as **The Ayres** and, at the Ayres Visitor Centre, a whole wealth of information can be found about this fascinating part of the island. Amongst the inland heath moorland, a variety of species of birds can be found nesting whilst, on the pebbled beaches, can be seen terns. The offshore sandbanks provide a plentiful supply of food for both the diving gannets and the basking grey seals.

Andreas   Map 5 ref O2
14 miles N of Douglas on A17

Originally a Viking settlement, the village church contains intricately carved crosses dating back to the days of these early occupants. The church tower's jagged spire goes back to the 1940s when it was removed in case it proved to be dangerous to aircraft from the nearby wartime airfields.

Sulby
Map 5 ref O3

11 miles N of Douglas on A3

Situated in the heart of the island, the village lies on the famous TT course, a circular route on the island's roads that takes in Douglas, Ramsey, Kirk Michael, and St John's. There are several scenic and picturesque walks from the village which taken in **Sulby Glen** and **Tholt-y-Will Glen**, both of which are renowned beauty spots, and to the south, over moorland, to Sulby reservoir. Bird watchers, particularly, will enjoy the walks over the higher ground as it provides the opportunity to see hen harriers, kestrels, peregrines, and curlews.

Just outside Sulby, in the rural heart of the island, lies the distinctive **Ginger Hall Hotel**, so named as a previous landlord brewed ginger ale here. The building dates back to the late 1800s and is ideally situated for easy access to good trout and salmon fishing in Sulby River and it also lies at the start of a ramblers' walk to Laxey.

Ginger Hall Hotel

Owned and personally run by Linda Thompson, this small hotel caters for the family, even the pet, in a relaxed and friendly atmosphere. With a recently refurbished restaurant, open fires in the bar, the comfortable residents' lounge and swings and slides in the garden for the children, this is a super place for the family's holiday base. The bar is open all day, every day during the summer, and there are several real ales on tap. As the hotel is situated on the TT course, visitors will not be surprised to see a large display of motor-cycle pictures and prints on the walls. *Ginger Hall Hotel, Ballamamagh Road, Sulby, Isle of Man IM7 2HB Tel: 01624 897231*

Ballaugh   Map 5 ref N3
11 miles N of Douglas on A3

The village, which lies on the TT race course, is close to the island's most extensive area of marshland, the perfect habitat for a range of birds, including woodcock and grasshopper warbler, as well as be-ing the largest roost for hen harriers in Western Europe.

Situated right on the island's famous TT course, **The Raven Country Inn** and Raven's Nest Bistro dates back to 1741 and is, today, personally run by Doreen and Phillip Ashworth. The age of this impressive inn is reflected inside where, although changes have taken place over the years, many of the original features, such as the stone fireplace and the ceiling beams, remain. The inn is open all day, every day, and as well as serving a fine range of real ales, including the local brew, a range of bar snacks are available at lunch-time.

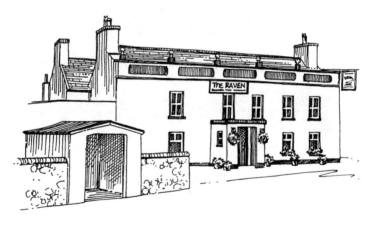

The Raven Country Inn
and Raven Bistro

An old converted barn, adjacent to the inn, is now home to the **Raven's Nest Bistro**, a popular restaurant that offers excellent meals in a cosy intimate setting. Open for dinner on Friday and Saturday evenings and for lunches on Sundays, for which it is necessary to book, the bistro has gained an enviable reputation that spreads throughout the island. The menu, which changes regularly, offers customers the very best of local ingredients that are presented in an interesting and imaginative manner that are sure to delight even the most discerning of guests. *The Raven Country Inn and Raven's Nest Bistro, Ballaugh Bridge, Ballaugh, Isle of Man IM7 5EG Tel: 01624 897272*

Situated on the edge of the Ballaugh Curraghs, **Curraghs Wildlife Park** is home to a wide variety of wetland wildlife that come from all over the world. Curraghs is the Manx word for the wet, boggy, willow woodland that is typical of this part of the island and the site, which was opened in 1965, gives visitors the opportunity to see the animals in the natural environments. This world renowned wildlife park has been divided into several different habitats, including The Pampas, The Swamp, The Marsh, and the Flooded Forest, and here endangered animals from around the world, such as Canadian otters, Spider monkeys, Rhea, and Muntjac deer, live as they would in the wild.

Curraghs Wildlife Park

The Curraghs Wildlife Park also has an enviable breeding record and, as many of the species are becoming rare in the wild, this is a very important aspect of the park's work. Not only have they successfully bred bald ibis, one of the most endangered birds in the world, but tapirs, lechwe antelope and many others also flourish in this environment. However, not all the animals and birds are exotic and there are a great number of native species to be seen here too.

Visitors to the park are able to wander around the various habitats, following a well laid path, and, with the aid of the well illustrated brochure the whole family will find this an interesting and informative trail. There is also an adventure play area for young children and, during the summer, a miniature railway runs around the park. The lakeside café is open during the day for refreshments and, during the main summer season when the park is open until 21.00, there is a barbecue. *Curraghs Wildlife Park, Ballaugh, Isle of Man IM7 5EA Tel: 01624 897323*

Kirk Michael
Map 5 ref N3
10 miles N of Douglas on A3

Close to the village lies **Glen Wyllin**, another of the island's 17 National Glens, and one that certainly deserves exploration. Kirk Michael also lies on a 16 mile footpath that follows the route of an old railway line from Peel to Ramsey. After following the coast, and part of the Raad ny Foillan, the footpath branches off through pastoral countryside before reaching the port of Ramsey on the other side of the island.

From its elevated position, 625 feet above sea level, the views from **Sartfield Farmhouse** are panoramic. Not only the island's western coast but, on a clear day, the Mountains of Mourne in Northern Ireland and the Mull of Galloway in Scotland, make an

Sartfield Farmhouse

impressive sight. When Barrie and Sandy Rose bought Sartfield in 1990, this 200 year old building was in need of a complete refurbishment. Although the premises had been used as a café for 40 years, it was their work and the addition of a large conservatory which turned Sartfield into the popular restaurant found today. Cosy and with a warm, friendly atmosphere, the restaurant has quickly established a reputation for quality home-cooked food, at prices to suit all pockets. As the island's 1998 Salon Culinaire Gold Medal winners for afternoon tea this is certainly the place to visit. Open every day except non-Bank Holiday Mondays, booking is essential for Sunday lunch (traditional roast), weekends, and race weeks. *Sartfield Farmhouse, Barre Garrow, Kirk Michael, Isle of Man IM6 1BE Tel: 01624 878280*

West of Douglas

Peel   *Map 5 ref M4*
9 miles W of Douglas on A1

On the western side of the island, it is generally felt that Peel, which is renowned for its sunsets, typifies the unique character and atmosphere of the Isle of Man. Traditionally the centre of the Manx fishing industry, including the delicious oak smoked kippers and fresh shellfish, Peel has managed to avoid any large scale developments. Its narrow winding streets exude history and draw the visitor unfailingly down to the harbour, sandy beach, and magnificent castle of local red sandstone.

Peel Castle, one of Isle of Man's principle historic monuments, occupies the important site of *St Patrick's Isle*. The imposing curtain wall encircles many ruined buildings, including St Patrick's Church, the 11th-century Round Tower, the 13th century Cathedral of St German, and the later apartments of the Lords of Man. In the 11th century the castle became the ruling seat of the Norse Kingdom of Man and the Isles, first united by Godred Crovan - the King Orry of Manx folklore.

Recent archaeological excavations have discovered exciting new evidence relating to the long history of the site. One of the most

Peel Castle

dramatic finds was the Norse grave of a lady of high social status buried in pagan splendour. The jewellery and effects buried with her can be seen on display, with other excavation finds, at the Manx Museum. The castle is also said to be haunted by the Black Dog, or Mauthe Dhoo, and, on dark windy nights, it can be heard howling in the castle's dungeons.

The Creek Inn, overlooking Peel's quay, has been owned and personally run by Jean and Robert McAleer for over 20 years and the licensing trade must be in the blood as both Robert's parents and grandparents were also publicans on the island. This attractive inn dates back over 250 years and, at one time, it was known as the Station Hotel. However, it took its present name in 1964 when

The Creek Inn

the railway line from Port Erin to Peel was closed. Not everything from the days of the railway have vanished though as, inside this stylish pub, there are several items left over from those days including a wonderful mirror showing the old railway. Open all day, every day, not only is there a fine range of drinks available, including the local brew, O'Kells, but a delicious menu of meals and bar snacks are served. Fish features heavily on the menu and, as might be expected, it is some of the freshest found anywhere in Britain. However, this is not all The Creek Inn has to offer the visitor as there are four comfortable self-catering apartments above the pub that have glorious views out to sea. *The Creek Inn, The Quay, Peel, Isle of Man IM5 1AT Tel: 01624 842216 Fax: 01624 843359*

Glenmaye   *Map 5 ref M4*
9 miles W of Douglas on A27

A spectacular bridged gorge and waterfall dominate this glen which is one of the most picturesque on the island. Comprising over 11 acres, its beautiful sheltered woodland includes some relics of the ancient forests that once covered much of the Isle of Man. Another feature of this glen is the Mona Erin, another of the many waterwheels which once produced power for the Manx lead mines.

Port Erin   *Map 5 ref L6*
12 miles W of Douglas on A5

Situated between magnificent headlands, Port Erin's beach is certainly a safe haven. It is also a place of soft sands cleaned daily by the tide with rock pools to one side and a quay to the other.

Visitors to the island may already have tasted the delicious breads, cakes, and pastries of **La Patisserie** without visiting the café as this is also a bakery which supplies many of the island's hotels, as well as Manx airlines, with fresh, home-baked foods. Open every day, except Sunday, the café offers an extensive menu of sandwiches, filled rolls and baguettes, and a wide range of cakes and pastries. Very popular with islanders, this is certainly a place not

La Patisserie

to be missed by those who enjoy fresh food, that is literally straight from the oven. With many of the ingredients, including authentic baguette flour, coming from France, La Patisserie offers customers a true Continental flavour. *La Patisserie, 21 Church Road, Port Erin, Isle of Man IM9 6AQ Tel: 01624 832254*

Calf of Man
15 miles W of Douglas

Map 5 ref L6

This small island, situated just off the southwestern tip of the island, is now a bird sanctuary owned by the National Trust. However, one of the previous owners, the Dukes of Athol, requested that the tenants living on the Calf pickled the nesting puffins! In 1777, a stone was found on the isle in the garden of Jane's Cottage, though in those days it was called The Mansion. Known as the Calf Crucifixion Cross, the stone is believed to date from the 8th century and it is one of the earliest Christian finds in Europe. The cross can be seen in the Manx Museum.

Calf Sound, the stretch of water between the island and the Isle of Man has seen many ships pass through and it was here that the largest armada of Viking longships ever assembled in the British Isles congregated before setting off to invade Ireland. Men from nearby Port St Mary were granted a gallantry medal by Napoleon, thought to be the only such medal he presented to British subjects, when they came to the rescue of the crew of the *St Charles* schooner from France which floundered in the sound.

Cregneash
13 miles W of Douglas off A31

Map 5 ref L6

Perched right on the southwestern tip of the island this village is now a living museum, **Cregneash Village Folk Museum**, which offers a unique experience of Manx traditional life within a 19th-century crofting community. Its isolated position led the village to become one of the last strongholds of the island's ancient skills and customs and all this is beautifully preserved today.

By combining small scale farming with other occupations, a small settlement of Manx men and women have successfully prospered here since the mid-1600s and, in the carefully restored buildings, visitors can see the conditions in which they lived and managed to sustain life in the this rugged landscape. The centrepiece of Cregneash is without doubt **Harry Kelly's Cottage**. Kelly was a renowned Cregneash crofter and a fluent speaker of the Manx language who died in 1934. Opened to the public in 1938, his cottage, still filled with his furniture, is an excellent starting point to any tour of the village. There are various other buildings of interest, including Turner's Shed, a smithy, and the Karran Farm.

The village is also one of the few remaining places where visitors get a chance to view the unusual Manx Loaghtan four-horned sheep, a breed which, thanks to Manx National Heritage and other interest groups, now has a secure future.

Port St Mary
Map 5 ref M6
12 miles W of Douglas off A31

This small working port has both an inner and outer harbour, two piers, and excellent anchorage for visiting yachts. The beach, along a scenic walkway from the harbour, is no more than two miles from the beach at Port Erin but it faces in almost the opposite direct and lies in the most sheltered part of the island.

One of the finest walks on the Isle of Man is the cliff top route from Port St Mary to Port Erin along the **Raad ny Foillan** - the road of the gull - a long distance footpath that follows the coastline right around the island. From Port St Mary, the first part of the walk takes in **The Chasms**, gigantic vertical rifts that, in some places, descend the full 400 feet of the cliffs.

As might be expected from its name, **The Shore** pub stands on the coast just outside the centre of Port St Mary. Some 150 years old, this impressive building has been a well-known landmark for

The Shore

boats, and more recently planes, for many years. Today, The Shore, owned by Betty and Nick Carter, is managed by their daughter Sue Rathbone-Scott who, along with chef Tony Harris, has made this a popular place that is renowned for its excellent food and drink. Open all day, every day, not only can visitors expect a fine selection of drinks behind the bar but there is also an interesting and imaginative menu of meals and bar snacks served from noon until 16.00. Outside, there is an attractive patio and barbecue area and, on occasional Saturday nights, live music is laid on for guests' enjoyment. Those visiting the island may be interested in the bed and breakfast accommodation that is also available at this hospitable pub. *The Shore, Gansey, Port St Mary, Isle of Man IM9 5LZ Tel: 01624 832269*

Castletown
Map 5 ref M6

9 miles W of Douglas on A7

The original capital of the island, the town's harbour lies beneath the imposing battlements of the finely preserved **Castle Rushen**. Like Peel Castle, this too is said to the haunted, by a ghost known as the White Lady. Believed to be the ghost of Lady Jane Gray who travelled to the island from Scotland with her family, she has been seen walking the battlements at night and occasionally walking through the castle's closed main gate during the day.

Dating back to 1153, the castle's construction was begun by Norsemen. A series of fascinating displays here bring the history and atmosphere of this great fortress vividly alive, by presenting in authentic detail the sights, sounds, and smells of its heyday. Among the various points of interest is a unique one-fingered clock that was presented to the castle by Elizabeth I in 1597 and which still keeps perfect time.

Castletown is also home to the island's **Nautical Museum**, where the displays centre around the late 18th century armed yacht *Peggy* which sits in her contemporary boathouse. Part of the original building is constructed as a cabin room from the time of the Battle of Trafalgar and there are many other artefacts on display all with a maritime theme.

On the road between Castletown and Douglas, visitors should look out for the **Fairy Bridge**. For centuries, people on the Isle of Man have taken no chances when it comes to the little people and it is still customary to wish the fairies who live under the bridge a Good Morning when crossing.

Situated opposite Castle Rushen, in the basement of an 18th-century building, is **The Keys Restaurant** which is owned and

The Keys Restaurant

personally run by Sue and John Olerenshaw. Cosy and intimate, with stone-faced walls and low ceiling beams, this charming restaurant offers diners an exciting menu of interesting dishes which John, the chef of the partnership, prepares from fresh ingredients. Open for both lunch and in the evening every day except Sundays, it is essential to book a table at this small restaurant to avoid disappointment. *The Keys Restaurant, Parliament Square, Castletown, Isle of Man IM9 1LA Tel: 01624 824000*

Near to Castletown's railway station and steam halt, is **The Sidings**, a popular inn that is housed in the attractive late 19th century former Castletown railway station building. Owned by Norman and Joy Turner and their partner David Quayle, this superb place at-

The Sidings

tracts visitors not just because of its superb position and history but also for is excellent fine food and drink. Open all day, the interior of the pub is as charming as is exterior, with many prints of the old and still running steam railway, its engines and its buildings. As well as serving a first class range of real ales, including the local favourite Webster's, The Sidings serves a delicious menu of tasty, freshly prepared dishes at both lunchtime and in the evening. To the rear of the building, adjacent to the railway line, is a delightful beer garden: a safe place for the children to play and also for steam enthusiasts to watch the trains go by. There can be few pubs in Britain which offer this interesting combination of superb attractions. *The Sidings, Station Road, Castletown, Isle of Man IM9 1EF Tel: 01624 823282*

Tourist Information Centres

Centres in **bold** are open all the year around.

Accrington
Town Hall, Blackburn Road, Accrington, Lancashire, BB5 1LA
Tel: 01254 386807 Fax: 01254 380291

Barnoldswick
The Council Shop, Fernlea Avenue, Barnoldswick, Lancashire
BB8 5DL Tel & Fax: 01282 666704

Blackburn
King George's Hall, Northgate, Blackburn, Lancashire, BB2 1AA
Tel: 01254 53277 Fax: 01254 683536

Blackpool
1 Clifton Street, Blackpool, Lancashire, FY1 1LY
Tel: 01253 478222 Fax: 01253 478210

Blackpool Pleasure Beach
Unit 25, Ocean Boulevard, Blackpool, Lancashire, FY4 1PL
Tel: 01253 403223 Fax: 01253 408718

Bolton
Town Hall, Victoria Square, Bolton, Greater Manchester
BL1 1RU Tel: 01204 364333 Fax: 01204 398101

Burnley
Burnley Mechanics, Manchester Road, Burnley, Lancashire
BB11 1JA Tel: 01282 455485 Fax: 01282 457428

Bury
The Met Arts Centre, Market Street, Bury, Lancashire, BL9 0BN
Tel: 0161 253 5111 Fax: 0161 253 5919

Cleveleys
Victoria Square, Thornton, Cleveleys, Lancashire, FY5 1AU
Tel: 01253 853378 Fax: 01253 866124

Clitheroe
12-14 Market Place, Clitheroe, Lancashire, BB7 2DA
Tel: 01200 425566 Fax: 01200 426339

Douglas
Sea Terminal, Douglas, Isle of Man, IM1 2RH
Tel: 01624 686766 Fax: 01624 627443

Fleetwood
Old Ferry Office, The Esplanade, Fleetwood, Lancashire
FY7 6DL Tel: 01253 773953 Fax: 01253 899000

Garstang
Discovery Centre, Council Offices, High Street, Garstang
Lancashire, PR3 1FU Tel: 01995 602125 Fax: 01253 899000

Lancaster
29 Castle Hill, Lancaster, Lancashire, LA1 1YN
Tel: 01524 32878 Fax: 01524 847472

Lytham St Annes
290 Clifton Drive South, Lytham St Annes, Lancashire, FY8 1LH
Tel: 01253 725610 Fax: 01253 713754

Morecambe
Station Buildings, Central promenade, Morecambe, Lancashire
LA3 2BT Tel: 01524 582808/582809 Fax: 01524 832745

Nelson
Town Hall, Market Street, Nelson, Lancashire, BB9 7LG
Tel: 01282 692890 Fax: 01282 695180

Onchan
Village Commissioners, Public Library, 61-69 Main Road, Onchan
Isle of Man IM3 1AJ Tel: 01624 621228

Peel
Town Commissioners Office, Town Hall, Derby Road, Peel, Isle of
Man, IM5 1HH
Tel: 01624 842341 Fax: 01624 836169

Port Erin
Commissioners Office, Station Road, Port Erin, Isle of Man
IM6 6AE Tel: 01624 842298 Fax: 01624 836169

Port St Mary
Commissioners Office, Town Hall, Port St Mary, Isle of Man
IM9 5DA Tel: 01624 832101 Fax: 01624 836267

Preston

The Guildhall, Lancaster Road, Preston, Lancashire, PR1 1HT
Tel & Fax: 01772 253731

Ramsey

The Library, Town Hall, Ramsey, Isle of Man, IM8 1AB
Tel: 01624 812228 Fax: 01624 813392

Rawtenstall

41/45 Kay Street, Rawtenstall, Rossendale, Lancashire, BB4 7LS
Tel & Fax: 01706 226590

Rochdale

The Clock Tower, Town Hall, Rochdale, Lancashire, OL16 1AB
Tel: 01706 356592

Southport

112 Lord Street, Southport, Merseyside, PR8 1NY
Tel: 01704 533333

Wigan

Trencherfield Mill, Wallgate, Wigan. Greater Manchester
WN3 4EL Tel & Fax: 01942 825677

Index

C

The Hidden Places Series

ORDER FORM

To order more copies of this title or any of the others in this series
please complete the order form below and send to:

**Travel Publishing Ltd,7a Apollo House, Calleva Park
Aldermaston, Berks, RG7 8TN**

	Price	Quantity	Value
Regional Titles			
Channel Islands	£6.99	....	....
Cheshire	£7.99	....	....
Cornwall	£7.99	....	....
Devon	£7.99	....	....
Dorset, Hants & Isle of Wight	£4.95	....	....
East Anglia	£4.95	....	....
Gloucestershire	£6.99	....	....
Heart of England	£4.95	....	....
Kent	£7.99	....	....
Lancashire	£7.99	....	....
Lake District & Cumbria	£7.99	....	....
Northeast Yorkshire	£6.99	....	....
Northumberland & Durham	£6.99	....	....
Nottinghamshire	£6.99	....	....
Peak District	£6.99	....	....
Potteries	£6.99	....	....
Somerset	£6.99	....	....
South East	£4.95	....	....
South Wales	£4.95	....	....
Surrey	£6.99	....	....
Sussex	£6.99	....	....
Thames & Chilterns	£5.99	....	....
Welsh Borders	£5.99	....	....
Wiltshire	£6.99	....	....
Yorkshire Dales	£6.99	....	....
Set of any 5 Regional titles	**£25.00**	....	....
National Titles			
England	£9.99	....	....
Ireland	£8.99	....	....
Scotland	£8.99	....	....
Wales	£8.99	....	....
Set of all 4 National titles	**£28.00**	....	....
	TOTAL	_____	_____

**For orders of less than 4 copies please add £1 per book for
postage & packing. Orders over 4 copies P & P free.**

*PLEASE TURN OVER TO COMPLETE
PAYMENT DETAILS*

The Hidden Places Series
ORDER FORM
Please complete following details:

I wish to pay for this order by:

Cheque:	☐	Switch:	☐
Access:	☐	Visa:	☐

Either:

Card No: ☐☐☐ ☐☐☐☐ ☐☐☐☐ ☐☐☐

Expiry Date: ☐☐ ☐☐

Signature: ....

Or:

I enclose a cheque for £ .... made payable to Travel Publishing Ltd

NAME: ....

ADDRESS: ....

....

....

....

POSTCODE: ....

TEL NO: ....

Please send to: Travel Publishing Ltd
7a Apollo House
Calleva Park
Aldermaston
Berks, RG7 8TN

The Hidden Places Series
READER REACTION FORM

The Hidden Places research team would like to receive reader's comments on any visitor attractions or places reviewed in the book and also recommendations for suitable entries to be included in the next edition. This will help ensure that the *Hidden Places* series continues to provide its readers with useful information on the more interesting, unusual or unique features of each attraction or place ensuring that their stay in the local area is an enjoyable and stimulating experience.

To provide your comments or recommendations would you please complete the forms below as indicated and send to: **The Research Department, Travel Publishing Ltd., 7a Apollo House, Calleva Park, Aldermaston, Reading, RG7 8TN.**

Please tick as appropriate: Comments ☐ Recommendation ☐

Name of *"Hidden Place"*:

Address:

Telephone Number:

Name of Contact:

Comments/Reason for recommendation:

Name of Reader:

Address:

Telephone Number:

Map Section

The following pages of maps encompass the main cities, towns and geographical features of Lancashire and the Isle of Man as well as all the many interesting places featured in the guide. Distances are indicated by the use of scale bars located below each of the maps

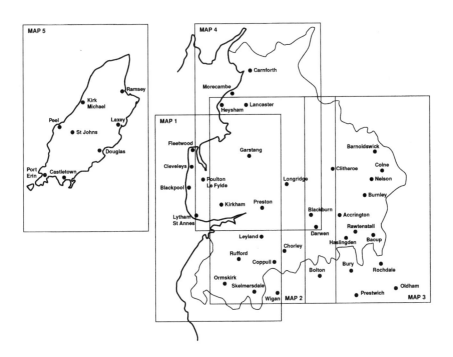

These maps are small scale extracts from the *North West England Official Tourist Map,* reproduced with kind permission of *Estates Publications.*

The Hidden Places of Lancashire

MAP 1

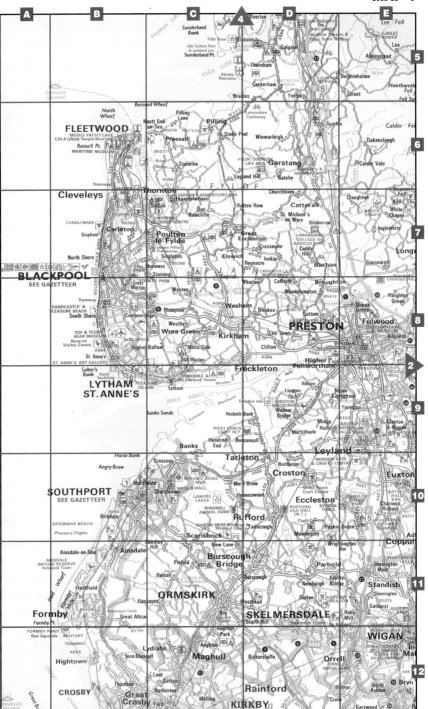

MAP 2

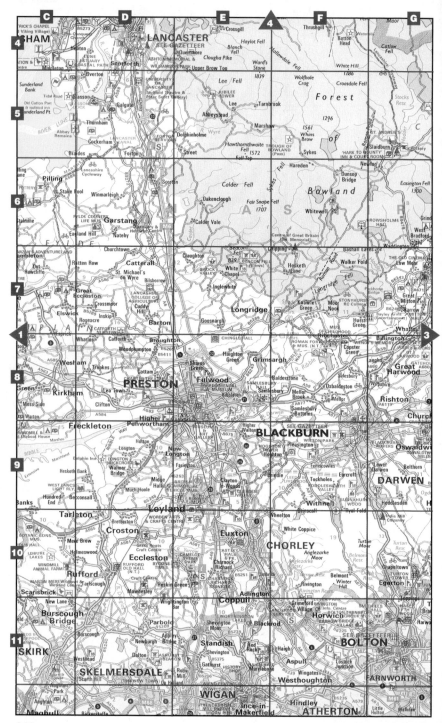

MAP 3

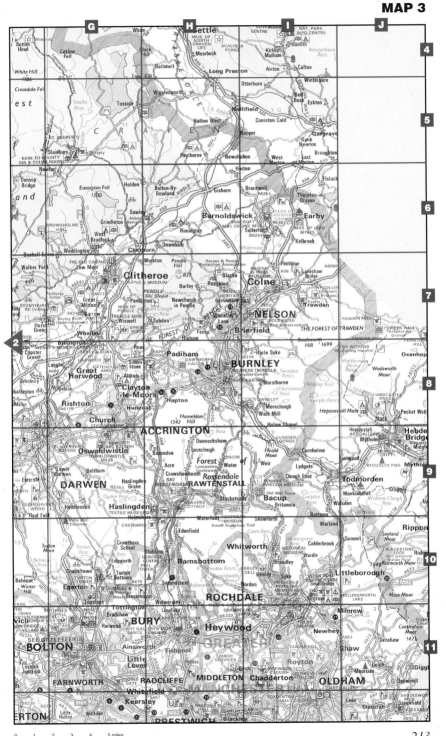

MAP 4

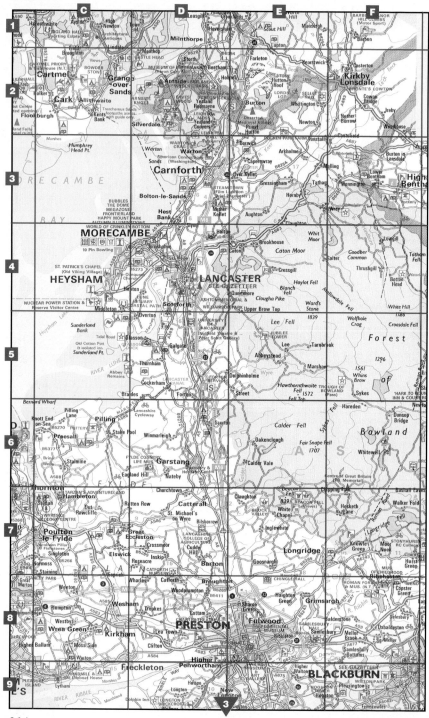

©Estate Publications   Crown Copyright Reserved

0 1 2 3 4 5 miles
0 1 2 3 4 5 6 7 8 kilometres

MAP 5

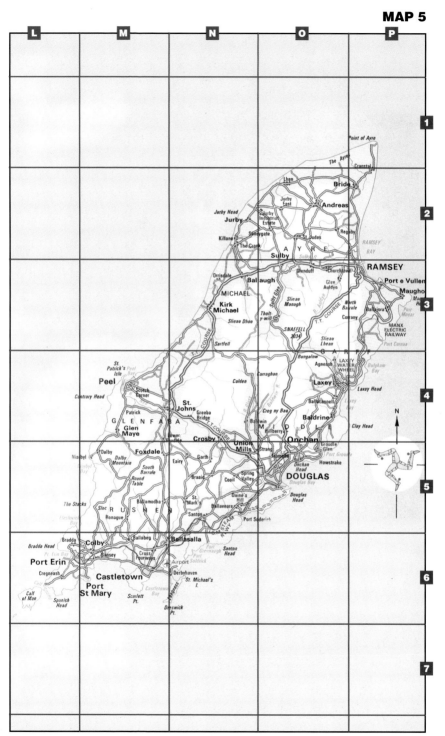